My Perfect Imperfections

How I Learned to Live in My Truth

DANA L. ROBERSON

PECAN TREE
PUBLISHING

New Voices, New Styles, New Vision
Empowering Authors with Impactful Stories
www.pecantreebooks.com
@pecantreepub – on all social media
Hollywood, FL

DEDICATION

Because of you, I know what pure, unwavering, unshakable love feels like. You will forever be my lifeline. Rest in peace, Mommy.

C O N T E N T S

INTRODUCTION

Some Days Are Life-altering

The day that I thought I closed my eyes for the very last time was the same day that my eyes were opened to a new life and a new beginning. I closed my eyes to my old world; the old me; only to awaken to a newness and an awareness that was terrifying, strange, and almost too big to accept. But I could finally breathe. A weight had finally been lifted. I would finally have answers and the right tools to help me live my best life possible. You could have never paid me to believe it would ever be me on the other side of an interview with an intake coordinator of a psychiatric unit.

It started after I went through my divorce in 2008. I had only been married for four years, but we had been together (on and off) for seven years. I was 19 years old; he was 21, and we met in college. The relationship had been extremely tumultuous, to say the least. It was doomed from the start. I must say this to clear the air. I've learned to be completely honest with myself about my life and if I'm going to tell this story, I've got to tell it right. I knew that I shouldn't have married this man. I'll tell you why I did – I wanted my family to work. We had a son out of wedlock two years prior to getting married; and felt marriage was the right thing to do. I think we both knew that it was not going to fix our problems, but somehow the thought of being married solidified things between us. We fell victim to the societal and religious beliefs

ix

surrounding us. It made things official. It would finally make us a family, right? Wrong! Prior to us getting married, there had been years of lying, hiding stuff, and lots of infidelity. I believed this man each time he cried, apologized, and promised not to "do it again." However, the cheating got even worse, the disrespect was amplified, and the distance grew even wider once we were officially married. We both came from stable homes and we both valued our families, however, what we brought to the relationship was a lot of confusion, uncertainty, and lack of knowledge on how to build and sustain a happy, healthy bond.

This was made evident by the lack of leadership from my husband and his inability to love me properly. I was responsible for taking care of everything related to the upkeep of the home (grocery shopping, cooking, cleaning, laundry, and similar tasks) plus taking our son to daycare and picking him up on most days. My husband's career trumped mine because he earned more money. He convinced me that I was responsible for the rest. It was an unfair dynamic for sure. Ultimately, he was in charge of our finances and my entire paycheck went to our savings account.

Several years into our marriage, I discovered that my husband had moved over 60 thousand dollars into a money market account without my knowledge and he claimed that he "tried to add my name to the account but could not." There were times I had to beg him to assist me around the house. It was a constant battle of trying to understand my purpose. I saw my dad work and provide for our family growing up and I saw my mom as the homemaker. I saw my role as the homemaker, and I was becoming increasingly frustrated with trying to force my husband to step into his role as provider and leader of our home. He mastered the financial side of things, however, he failed tremendously at being present emotionally. I take full responsibility for allowing that dynamic to go on for as long as it did.

Like a lot of couples, we sought comfort in going to church. What's that old cliché? "A family that prays together, stays together." Well, we prayed together, alright. The problem was, as soon as we were done praying, he would leave our son and I to go to the movies, hang out with his friends, go to the gym, you name it. It's as if he always had somewhere else to be other than at home with me and our son. I allowed this to happen because it's exactly what I saw growing up. My dad would work in his grocery store all day long, come home, shower, and then go hang out. I had accepted that this is what men do. I felt angry for allowing my ex to treat me so poorly, but over time I would learn even more about the depths of my low self-esteem and poor self-image. Had I been confident and had I loved myself just a tiny bit, I could have walked away from the cycle of abuse sooner.

My low self-esteem wasn't very noticeable to others around me, but I can remember not loving myself as a child or a young adult. I was the middle child of five and I came out of the womb competing for attention. I don't think it was that I lacked attention, I always wanted good attention. You know, the attention you get for doing good things? Perfectionism set in for me at a young age and it ruled my life well into my 40s. There was no specific incident that caused my inability to forgive myself or believe in myself; it came from somewhere internal. My first addiction was people pleasing, and the sad part is that it was an unattainable goal. I constantly paid attention to the mood of others believing that my actions attributed to their happiness or displeasure. I had a responsibility to make others happy when I was in their presence. I lived my life going as far as I needed to go to make sure others were okay. Eventually, I learned that this was detrimental to me in a varying way. It was exhausting and it caused unnecessary self-judgment, and a lack of confidence. The words on repeat in my head for years were, "I hope they like it" or "I hope he likes me." My perspectives during my youth and my posture in my relationship were the breeding ground for depression, anxiety, and other mental health issues.

I found out about his infidelity three months after we were married. I had already known he was a cheater, but I chose to give him a chance. He had cheated within six months of our meeting, so I knew what I was signing up for. The young lady he cheated with in college approached me, uninvited, and shared the details of her whirlwind love affair with him. I remember he cried and denied his infidelity for hours; and then he bought me a puppy. Yep, a cute white, fluffy shih tzu that I named Puffy. The first argument we had after he graced me with that gift, Puffy was snatched from my arms, driven to Jacksonville, and given to his parents. If that wasn't a RED DAMN FLAG! But I stayed because he always promised, through the crocodile tears, that he would "never lie or cheat again." I trusted him. I believed his lies until the emails proved otherwise. My ex-husband always kept the same password for everything, so one day while I was at work, I decided to check his personal email. I hated snooping, but if you've ever been with someone who constantly lies and treats you like crap for no apparent reason, it's really a matter of gathering evidence. That thing we call our "gut" and the intuition that lies within is serious. I always trusted that weird feeling and it often led me right to the answers. I took a dive into his filthy emails and discovered that this man was having another affair. This time it was a woman that he had met while at a business meeting in Chicago. My heart pounded and the adrenaline pulsated as I read the exchanges between the two of them. He admitted to her that he was married, then I read the following sentence: "Yes, I am married, but I'm only with her for my son. I must be a part of my son's life no matter what." He went on to tell her how amazing it felt to "lay there staring into [her] eyes." She asked him if he "does this often because it's interesting that you travel with condoms in your luggage when you're a married man." I then saw emails confirming their upcoming trip to Vegas together. I literally saw the plane tickets! It was right there in my face. I knew I needed to act. I confronted him about this first episode. Of course, he lied. It's sad when you have hard-core, tangible evidence and the person you love stands before you and lies without emotion or concern. I was exhausted and our marriage was just getting started.

I ended up moving out of our home to prove a point. It was important for me to let this man know that I would not tolerate infidelity in our marriage. Moving out was me proving to him that I could make it on my own. This obviously stemmed from my childhood and what I promised myself I would never endure. I didn't want to manifest my mother's inability to move on with her life when things became more than tough with my dad. I witnessed years of her crying and being blatantly disrespected. It became part of my emotional DNA to fight back and be assertive if someone tried me.

Leaving my husband after the first few months of marriage was terrifying, to say the least. I was new to the city with a two-year-old and no family or friends. I was making 30 thousand dollars per year, and I didn't know how I was going to make it on my own. I did what I knew best, and I put in the work to create the life I wanted. However, my estranged husband had other plans. He wanted his family back and he was using every measure to make that happen. It didn't help that I had only moved less than one mile down the street. That was poor planning because he was at my apartment every night helping with our son's bath time and bedtime. He would bring gifts like a Tiffany's bracelet with matching necklace. He bought me flowers and perfume. He did any and everything to win my heart. It was only a matter of months before his lies, tears, begging, and pleading led me right back to our home with him. All the promises to do better were empty, yet I decided to trust him one more time.

This cycle reminds me of what I witnessed my mother go through emotionally. Not exactly in terms of leaving and returning, but I watched my mom cry on a few different occasions, and as a young child I believed that if he made you cry, then you should leave because that means he doesn't love you anymore. How I was able to interpret this at 11 years old is beyond me, but I somehow equated those tears with the need to move along. So, time after time when my mom didn't move along, I grew to resent that side of her. Why wasn't she strong enough to remove herself from that situation? As an adult, in my own tumultuous marriage, I was beating myself up for being that very same woman. I had to fight back because this lifestyle would surely kill me. There has always been this outspoken side to me that I can't let rest at times. It was at an all-time high at this time in my marriage. The biggest frustration for me at this time was coming to the realization that in as much as I thought I was avoiding the type of relationship that my parents had, I fell into the stereotypical outcome that most daughters have, and I ended up marrying someone just like my dad. Go figure!

A few months after I moved back home, the husband demanded that I go back to church with him and attend couple's counseling. I always wondered why my ass was being dragged to counseling for something he kept doing. This was the foundation of our marriage. Clearly not built on solid ground. Just a bunch of bullshit. Even the pastor got tired of my ex-husband's cheating. He literally stated to him in one of our sessions: "Ok, my brother, there's only so much I can do to help you. You must decide. If you cheat one more time, Dana has every right to leave this marriage."

That warning stuck for about 11 months. Enough time for my ex to make me think he'd made the changes and had put in the work, only to find that he was cheating again.

I spent a lot of time in my marriage trying to find strength. I have always been a spiritual person, so I "re-found" myself over and over a lot. I wrote in my journal each day; I had to find an outlet. I was trying to make sense of the mess that I had gotten myself into. I was not happy at all and none of this made sense. I was never taught how to be in a relationship with a man. My view of what marriage was supposed to be was warped. The marriages I saw on television or read about, didn't match up with the image of marriage I got from my parents. I witnessed a lot of infidelity and jacked up gender roles. Basically, my father was the breadwinner and sole provider. My parents had five kids together so there was a lot on my mother's plate. My parents are amazing, so don't get me wrong. They were basically living out their roles based on what they had seen growing up. My father is and has always been a very hard worker. He started picking oranges in the orange groves in order to make money while he was still in high school. His father, (my grandfather), instilled a strong work ethic in him and his eight siblings. My father left the house every morning at 5 a.m. to operate his corner grocery store and he didn't return home until 8:30 p.m.

My mom was a homemaker and took care of everything related to me and my siblings and everything related to the household. My mom was our chef, our chauffeur, our doctor, our nurse, our hair stylist, our confidante. My mother was also extremely obedient and loyal to a fault to my father.

All I knew was that I was trying to be perfect and have the perfect little marriage and family. My husband was making that impossible for me. Even though I wanted our perfect marriage to be a wonderful reality, the truth was it reminded me painfully of how I was always concerned about whether others were pleased with me. I was preoccupied with making others happy even if it meant I was miserable. If they were smiling and enjoying themselves, that's all that mattered to me. My earliest memory of being physically charged up at the compliments someone showered on me was in kindergarten. I remember showing Mrs. Berry a picture of a bright shiny apple I had drawn on a piece of construction paper with big chunky crayons. Her response stuck with me for the rest of my life because it ignited something in me. She gasped as she took the paper from my hand. She sat back in amazement and shouted, "My goodness! This apple is peeeeerfect, Dana!!!" My body burst into a full-on Fourth of July fireworks show from my head to my toes. I felt the excitement she exuded, and it was contagious. I had made her so proud of me just by creating this perfect little apple! I think I've spent the rest of my life chasing that type of high. That type of elatedness; that type of joy and happiness in others due to something thoughtful yet simple that I've done. It was my first addiction, for sure.

Unfortunately, I couldn't let people around me know what was going on in my marriage because the shame was too embarrassing. I know people would ask, "how could you be so stupid?" or "how could you be so weak?" I was angry at myself because I had always promised myself that I would never become this woman. I was independent, educated, and strong. I did not need my husband but for some reason, I stayed. I allowed this man to make me feel like I was unlovable, unwanted, and never enough for him. I sat on the sidelines and watched as he paraded around as if his life with me was perfect.

Meanwhile, I was crumbling inside. I was aching for attention. My inner hatred toward myself manifested in all sorts of ways, especially after seeing pictures of the women that he preferred over me. Especially after reading the emails in his own words, "I only got married because I want to be a part of my son's life." Those types of things cut deep like a knife. And yet, I stayed. I pretended. I think some part of me was up for the challenge of "being a good wife." Whatever the hell that meant.

Fast forward to four years later and being fed up. I had taken my annual trip to Jamaica and returned home only to find that my husband had lied to me for the last and final time. All it took this time was checking our online bank transactions while I was gone. I pieced things together and the truth was laid out before me and there was no denying that he had done it again. This was when I realized that his lies were not going to stop, and this cycle was going to continue. I made up in my mind that I would rather live homeless on the street if I had to (thankfully this was never the case) than to continue to live with this monster. When I confronted him that time, he threatened me. I will never forget the words he said to me, "Go ahead. Go out there and try to find another nigga like me!"

The next day he was sobbing like a baby when he realized I was leaving everything behind. I think we both knew this was finally it. There was no turning back for me - finally. As frightening as it was for me to step out in a city where I had no family or roots, I knew that I had to start over and make a life for me and my son. My future would not include the dark clouds of this man. I had finally found the strength and courage within me to break free.

I don't want to make it sound as if this transition was easy. It was the hardest thing to do, and I grappled with it for a long time. I spent many sleepless nights lying in bed crying. I shed tears because I was mourning the loss of something that I held dear to me. No matter how tumultuous things had been, this man was all I had ever known. I loved him from his head to the tip of his toenails. I loved him so hard and so much. We had a son together and I valued the idea of us being a family. I wanted so badly for us to be a happy little family. He knew how to win me back, but this time it wasn't working. When we were married, I had to beg this man to help me out around the house. He wouldn't even take the trash out, but as soon as I left, he showed up at my place volunteering to take my trash to the bin at the front of the apartment complex. I later found out he would go through my trash. Not only that, one day I was driving our kindergartner home from school, and I noticed he couldn't stay awake. We had him on a strict schedule, and he never fell asleep that time of the day. I asked my son what was wrong, and he said he was, "up late last night because we were at your apartment. Daddy told me to just lay down in the backseat, but I couldn't get comfortable." I flipped out! I called my husband and confronted him about this. Was this real? My ex told me that he was making sure I wasn't spending time with other men. It was an awful time.

I went to the police station the next day and asked what my options were because the man was making my life miserable. He had also had a friend of his pull my cell phone records, and he was calling all my friends, family, and coworkers on that list. I had a coworker call me and tell me that my ex interrogated him by phone! Another friend shared that my ex called him and told him we were trying to work things out, so it was best for him to avoid contact with me. I was floored! He did his normal routine of doing everything in his power to get me back, but he was going too far. Because we worked in the same industry, I had coworkers telling me what physicians (our customers in the pharmaceutical industry) were being told a variety of personal and professional untruths by my ex. He was spreading rumors to anyone who would listen. The word on the street was that I "left him because I wanted to start seeing other men." That must be the dumbest thing I'd ever heard, but guess what, I held my head up high. I never disputed the rumors because I knew the truth. All I could do was pray about that level of ignorance. But the truth of the matter is, it did affect me. I turned more inward after my divorce and my heart started to harden.

I sobbed when I thought about becoming another statistic. I hated the idea of being a single mother. I knew it was something I had to do, though. I had to face the music. I had to acknowledge my own mistakes and get the hell out of there! The thoughts that wouldn't leave me alone and that haunted me for years are the ones that I fought with the most, "no one loves you", "you're not good enough", "what makes you think you can keep a man happy?" I thought that I had done everything right. I was my husband's biggest cheerleader and fan. I encouraged him, poured into him, and supported all his wildest dreams. I prayed for him. I cooked. I kept our house clean. I went to the gym and kept my body fit. I kept my hair and nails done. I took care of our son. I was available to my husband whenever, WHEREVER he wanted me. And I was lost and confused as I looked back and tried to figure out what I had done wrong. It would take me years to realize it had never had anything to do with me.

Once I moved out, one of the best pieces of advice a friend gave me was that I should wait 90 days before I filed for the divorce. Although things were ugly between my husband and I, and it was obvious that divorce was the right thing to do, it was a way of being absolute. I left him in February 2008, filed in May, and the divorce was finalized on the day before my son's sixth birthday in October. We didn't fight much over anything because I made everything simple. I made it abundantly clear that I didn't want anything from my ex-husband. I didn't want the house, the car, the furniture; hell, I didn't even want alimony or child support! I wanted my freedom. My ex-husband had so much control in our relationship that when we got married, he picked out our new pre-construction home, he picked out all the new furniture and chose the color of the walls. It was pointless for me to share my ideas, opinions, or likes about anything because he would shoot me down and eventually, we'd land on whatever he liked best. I wanted to be rid of all my ties to him. But of course, raising a son together meant that we would have to coordinate our schedules and work out the best plan for our son. We amicably agreed to a 50/50 schedule where my son would be with both parents every week and each parent every other weekend. My son was six years old at the time of the divorce. He is an adult now, and things with him are turning out amazing. We've all had our moments where things got tough, but we worked through it as a family in our own unique way.

For the most part, my ex-husband and I grew to put our son's needs first. We put our differences aside and we learned to become partners in parenting our son into a decent young man. In the beginning, I typed out our son's schedule, which included when his lunch funds and after school care fees were due. It included details on his practice schedule when he played sports and did Taekwondo. I was on top of keeping us organized. It was frustrating at times because just as he had behaved in our marriage, he often took a backseat when it came to the heavy lifting. For instance, I oversaw taking our son to orientation before the first day of school each year. I physically went and purchased all his school supplies every year and all my ex had to do was pay half after I sent him the receipt. I remember by 6th or 7th grade, I texted my ex and told him he needed to take care of orientation and school supplies that year. He almost died and he was so angry at me. I had made things so easy for him and he was pissed. I didn't back down and it was for the best because I should have operated like this from day one. He was not paying child support and we were splitting custody 50/50 so that meant he needed to physically do his part, as well. When I realized this, I had no problem holding my ex accountable.

I like to think that we've become friends again. That's hard to say. I know we don't hate one another. There's more love there than anything. We recognize our mistakes, and I can say this because I don't blame him for everything that went wrong in our marriage. As I said before, I knew who he was and how he was before I married him, therefore, I played a role in the demise of my marriage, too. In no way am I making excuses for the things that happened. I have learned that facing the truth is the quickest way to heal. There were days of co-parenting when I thought for sure we wouldn't make it. The things we fought about the most were issues concerning my son's school. My ex fought for top-tier education, while I was fine with the neighborhood schools, which in our case, were all "A" schools. In retrospect, I can appreciate how these programs truly did set my son apart. I still feel strongly about the school systems in the United States, but that's a different book. We had to coordinate everything and when two adults are trying to rebuild separate lives with a child and their needs at the core, it's a hell of an experience, which is less about the divorce, and more about the responsibility and the sacrifice each person must make. I applaud divorcing couples with more than one child. In hindsight, I'm thankful we were never on the same page regarding having more kids. I'm thankful for our son and all that he taught us as his parents. Although the marriage didn't work out, we will always be a family unit.

A wealth of things has happened between then and now. Which is what this book is about. It reflects the years after my divorce that led me down an unhealthy road of self-destruction. I wanted to write this book as a part of my healing, but also to help others avoid the pitfalls of this treacherous journey. There are more healthy ways to deal with life's challenges, especially when things seem hopeless. I plan to share my journey and the resources that provided help which allowed me to rebuild my life again. I admit this walk down memory lane was quite painful for me, but I know that it is my duty to share so that at least one life might be touched, healed, or saved.

C H A P T E R   1

My First Depression

I was still married when I was first diagnosed with depression. It was during the first two months when my then husband cheated on me, and I found out. I thought I had finally gotten things right in my life when suddenly, my marriage came crumbling down around me. Of course, this didn't happen over-night, but that is sure as hell what it felt like. All I know is that one day I woke up alone, in my bed with my covers pulled over my head and I was unable to move. Literally, unable to move. I felt like the weight of the world was hovering over my covers and the sad and sickening thing about it is that I was amazingly comfortable there. I did not want to move. I wanted to stay there forever. That is what depression felt like for me. It was dark, it was quiet, it was desolating, and it was comforting.

I had moved out of our apartment and tried to move away from him. I was so broken because I knew I had made the biggest mistake of my life by marrying this man. Like I said before, I knew he was a cheater so the fact that I had caught him red handed came to no surprise. I found myself unable to sleep or eat. I felt numb. Eventually, this took a toll on my body, and I became ill. I was calling in sick to work because of "sore throats and body aches." I felt like I was going to die. Literally. One day, during our separation, my husband came to my apartment and took me to the doctor. The doctor was a friend of his. I felt like it was a waste of time. I knew that all I needed was a good night's sleep and I would be fine. Boy was I wrong.

Once at the doctor's office, I sat in the cold room waiting for the doctor to come in. My cheating husband sat across from me. A look of concern on his face. All he wanted was for me to come back home. *Lying bastard….*is all I could think. The doctor finally came in. Questions were asked about my medical history. Then he asked about my current situation. He didn't realize that my husband and I were separated. He asked my husband to leave the room. There was something in the way this doctor stood before me and held my hands and asked me to "let it out." It's like a flood gate was opened. I began to cry uncontrollably. I told him how I was falling apart and how I couldn't get out of bed, not even to give my three-year-old son a bath. I felt like a horrible mother. I felt like a failure because I had trusted this man and his lies. I felt embarrassed because everyone would know that our marriage was a joke. *I mean who gets married and cheated on after just two months?!? I wanted to crawl into a hole and never come out again!*

The doctor consoled me. He gently wiped my tears, and he said the words that I'll never forget. *"Sweetie, you're just going through a mild depression right now. It will pass. I have something that will help you."*

At the time, I was working as a clinical therapist, so I knew exactly what he meant. That meant it was time for a low dose of medication if I was open to it. The way I felt at that moment and in the weeks leading up to it, I was open to anything. I wanted my life back. I wanted to see the sunshine again. I wanted to feel hope again. I wanted to feel like I could make it through that and any rough patch. The doctor gave me a week's worth of samples and wrote me a prescription. He told me that he wanted to see me back in two weeks. I felt better already.

That was 2004, the first time I was prescribed medication. I was willing to try the medication because my doctor told me that my depression was situational. That seemed to provide some level of comfort to me. I was terrified that I would have to take medication for the rest of my life. Amid depression, nothing seems positive and the thought of ever being normal again is a million miles away. To hear that this trial with medication was only for a short while and that I should feel better within two weeks, I was willing to do whatever it took. Besides, my son needed me. My job needed me. My family needed me. My friends needed me. Even my cheating ass husband *NEEDED* me. The list of reasons why can go on and on, but you get the picture.

Within a few short days of starting my medication, I felt like a different person. I could think more clearly and handle my emotions a lot better. I was sleeping better and crying a lot less. I was showing up to work and performing my job functions again and I was present in my son's life, which was the most important part to me. Things between my husband and I were starting to get better since he had convinced me to go to couple's counseling with our pastor at our church. I wanted more than anything to save my marriage. I was willing to do everything in my power to salvage our young marriage. I would be willing to do the work if he was too. So that's what we did. I moved back home three months later.

I mention my first experience with depression because it is important in my overall story. Depression strikes in episodes. According to the Diagnostic and Statistical Manual of Mental Disorders (DSM-IV), "the essential feature of a Major Depressive Episode is a period of at least 2 weeks during which there is either depressed mood or the loss of interest or pleasure in nearly all activities. The individual must experience at least four additional symptoms drawn from a list that include changes in appetite or weight, sleep, and psychomotor activity; decreased energy; feelings of worthlessness or guilt; difficulty thinking, concentrating, or making decisions; or recurrent thoughts of death or suicidal ideation, plans, or attempts." I was in a living hell with the majority of these symptoms.

But I finally felt alive again. My family and friends were cheering for my marriage and their support felt great. No one knew, however, about the darkness of my depression. That was something I kept secret. The only thing people knew was that

I was strong and that I was fighting for my family. That's all I would allow them to see. No one saw the nights when I would come home from work, exhausted, and bury my head in my pillow and scream, with tears running down my face. Still hurt from the betrayal, the words, *"I'm only with her because I promised I would never leave my son"* haunted me day and night. Knowing that was the real reason my husband was sticking around angered me. Yet he pretended as if I had something to do with it....as if it were really love that kept him there. It was all a game.

One thing that came out in counseling was that we were caught in a vicious cycle. My husband had a side to him that I could never explain to others. It was an unspoken hatred toward me that confused me. His actions did not match up with his words. On the one hand he adored me - when it was convenient for him. On the other hand, if it was inconvenient or not beneficial to him, then I was just like everyone else. I never felt special or chosen. I was always competing with other women. I was in a living hell because part of me knew that I was being mistreated and deserved more; yet I was afraid to start over after investing so much time, energy, resources, and love into the relationship. One night during a counseling session, our pastor asked us to each write down the one thing we were afraid of in our marriage. I wrote down that I was afraid that my husband would cheat on me again. He wrote down that he was afraid that I would leave him again. We were simply two lost souls. Stuck in a vicious cycle. He would forever cheat. I would forever leave. Our marriage was doomed. But cheating was not the only thing that I would be worried about.

Knowing that we had these fears in our marriage caused a bigger rift between my husband and me. I was living in a world where he was already guilty of cheating. I was already packed with one foot out of the door most of the time. That's no way to live. Our marriage was never stable in this way. It's as if we were always looking over our shoulders. I was waiting for the other shoe to drop all the time. It was not a marriage built on trust. How could it be? I spent hours thinking the worst. Can you imagine living that way? It was torture.

When you live with a person who has had an affair, a super long list of questions is constantly swirling in your head. Where is he now? What lies will he tell next? Is he really going on another business trip alone? Why is he listening to love songs? He only likes hard-core hip-hop and rap music. Why is he going to the gym so much? Why can't I go with him this time? Why doesn't he look at me the same anymore? What did I ever do to deserve this? Why does this man hate me so much? Why is he such a liar? What can I do to make him love me more? Should I change my hair? Do I need to lose more weight? Do I need to talk softer? Louder? Do I complain too much? Am I getting on his nerves? Does he even like me?

All these questions, and more, can drive a person insane. I lived like that every day. I was desperate for him to love me back. I was desperate for affection, and this stemmed from years of not receiving the physical touch (unless we were intimate) I needed and receiving little to no affirmation. He claimed to not be the touchy-feely type and I accepted that. In hindsight I see that love languages are important and had I known that physical touch and affirmation are huge for me, I wouldn't have chosen this man. I was making a fool of myself by putting him and all his needs first. It was my mission to make him feel good. To make him happy. To make him proud of me as his wife. All the while, he had his own agenda. I'm willing to bet my husband saw nothing wrong. That's because he was living his best life with his cheerleader wife who took care of everything so that he could go out and be great. There was no end to it. It was utter torture. It drove me deeper and deeper into my depression and farther and farther away from myself. I didn't know who I was anymore. I didn't know what my purpose was. I was losing myself.

After four years of marriage, I fled. I knew I would have to be the one to leave. Otherwise, we'd probably still be married today. I was dying in my marriage. I can't pinpoint where my strength came from on that final day, but I had had enough. Once I returned from my annual trip to Jamaica, I found some discrepancies in his story about where he had been and who he had been with while I was away. I saw the evidence and for the last time, I said enough is enough. I confronted my husband, quietly packed my bags the next day and I left. It was amazing how simple that part was. I guess what they say is true – "When a woman's fed up, there ain't nothing you can do about it."

C H A P T E R   2

Life on My Own

Immediately after leaving my husband, I was wrought with fear. I would have to say my biggest fear was financial. How was I going to make it on my own? I had become so accustomed to our life together, never wanting for anything. Now, it was going to be different. I would have to start all over since I had walked away from everything. When I say everything, I mean EVERYTHING – the house, the car, the furniture, even the damn eating utensils!

I found an apartment that I could afford within a day of my decision to leave; and I made sure that I didn't have to disrupt my son's schooling. It was important for me that his life remained as stable as possible. The apartment was also close enough to my soon-to-be ex-husband so that we could share the responsibility of raising our son together. That was extremely important to my husband. I waited 90 days before I filed for divorce. I wanted to be 100% sure that I was absolutely done with the vicious cycle. I was done. Once I filed for divorce, the overwhelming feeling of "can I really go through with this?" set in.

The paperwork itself was enough to make me want to change my mind. All the line item details, all the questions, down to how much I paid for toilet paper each month! It was daunting, but I pushed through, and my attorney saw me through each step of the process. Financially, I sustained myself because by then I had switched careers and was working in the pharmaceutical industry.

I was making a nice salary plus bonuses. I had a company vehicle and fuel card. That was extremely helpful in terms of my monthly expenses. I am so thankful for my job because I know if it hadn't been for that security and flexibility, I probably would have crumbled. It was extremely expensive (thousands of dollars in fact) to pay for attorney fees and everything else that comes with those types of proceedings.

Thankfully, because I wasn't asking for much, my husband and I agreed to settle everything in mediation. This kept us from having to fight things out in court. We literally sat across a long table from one another with each of our attorneys present and went back and forth a few times on the appropriate schedule for our son (shared custody) and it was over. I cried myself to sleep that night for many reasons, including the end of our marriage happening, the day before my son's sixth birthday.

It was finally over between me and the man I had known since I was 19 years old and the only man I'd ever loved. I was 30 years old when the dissolution of the marriage happened. I was finally free from his lies and his hurt and pain. But I also realized in that moment that I was still his prisoner. You see, one thing I had agreed to in mediation was that since we would share custody, I would agree to live within 50 miles of my ex-husband. I had to agree to that and agree to get permission from him if I wanted to move until my son turned 18 years old. It was such a bittersweet experience. Free but not so free. I felt, in some ways, like I had signed my death sentence.

CHAPTER 3

Life Goes On

Picking up the pieces of my life did not take long for me. I was thriving at work, my son was doing well at school and playing sports. His teachers were aware of the divorce and were keeping his father and I abreast of any changes in his behavior. By this time, I had experienced my second episode of depression, had gotten the help that I needed and was off my medication. I had a great support network around me. I thought I was doing fine. For the most part, that's what it looked like.

Deep down inside I was still aching. There was a part of me that hadn't healed yet. There was a part of me that the medication couldn't reach. I knew that life was steadily moving all around me, and I was expected to keep up. The question became "how do I keep up?" I often felt like I was breaking down. I was exhausted from keeping up the façade that I was strong. I needed help and the type of help that I needed I didn't seek out. I started to drink socially with my friends on the nights that my son was with his dad. It was a way for me to pass the time. Girls' nights out were a must. The weekends that he spent with his dad were booked with trips with friends or visiting family. I couldn't sit still. I couldn't be alone.

Dating became a game. Because of my issues with trust, I never let anyone get too close. I would have my fun but as soon as a man would get too close to me, I would toss the grenade and blow that shit up right in his face. It was that simple. No one was going to ever crush me the way my ex-husband had. I started drinking more. The girls' nights out ended with me coming home to fix a night cap. In between the girls' nights, a busy workday called for coming home, kicking off my heels, and popping open a bottle of wine. Then I graduated to tequila shots and wine. Then it was straight vodka. I would mix Crystal Light, water, and Tito's vodka to make sure I didn't gain any weight. There was a method to the madness. Meanwhile, I was still thriving at work. Never skipping a beat with my responsibility to be a mother. My life was insane.

I often found myself in situations that I look back on today and wonder how I made it out alive. Seriously. I should have been dead a long time ago. I was living my life on the edge. I was living recklessly. I obviously didn't have a care in the world at a certain point. So long as my son was with his dad and safe, I was off doing my own thing trying to fill a void. A pit full of hurt that could never be filled by anything or anyone engulfed me. I never did any drugs, but the alcohol and the men were certainly there. It was enough to write an entire book about. [I'll spare you the details here, and I'll point you to my next book, which will be an exploration of my encounters and how those experiences shaped me. All things relationships, so stay tuned!]

Long story short, I was broken. I was damaged. I was wounded. I was walking around looking for the nearest hospital. The only problem is no one saw my brokenness. No one saw the blood. No one saw the wounds. I hid the hurt, guilt, and shame so well. No one could reach out to help me even if they tried. I probably would have turned them away. I hid behind a huge smile. I hid behind my humor. I hid behind my strength and my super mom cape. Meanwhile, every night I was going home, ripping the cape off, drowning in a fifth of vodka, and swimming in my tears. Alone.

I was alone on purpose. It was by design. I had secretly made up in my mind that I would never give myself away to a man the way I had with my ex. I made a promise to myself that I would never cater to a man in that same way. These decisions were being made during the worst pain of my life. That dull pain that is just there below the surface, aching, gnawing at you, and you can't seem to alleviate it. The idea of love was foreign to me at this point, so the goal was to NEVER get attached again.

Being alone was safe for me. It was the isolation that felt the best after a romp in the sheets with someone. I'd kick them out before they could even zip their pants up. I had zero desire for pillow talk, and I quickly became heartless. I could care less about the guys I spent time with and if I'm being honest, it was almost cathartic. As sick as it sounds, I was finding relief in pulling these men in and then pushing them away. Little did I know I was doing much more damage to myself than I was willing to admit. I was extremely erratic. I was hot and cold and the men in my world were the ones who caught my wrath. I can look back on several different scenarios where things didn't have to go as far as they did. It was never anything physical. My razor tongue was all I needed. It was my defense mechanism when I wanted to lash out. Whoever was in front of me in those moments was the one who got it. I was unleashing pain from my childhood. I was striking back at every man who had wronged me. I'm sure I left a lot of these men confused and I probably even hurt a few. That wasn't my problem. I really didn't care.

C H A P T E R   4

Tick-Tick-BOOM!

One can only pretend for so long. My nights started to turn to days, and I was running on empty all the time. I was exhausted. I never slept anymore. Years had gone by. I had moved into my own home a year after leaving my husband. I was one of the top performers at work, and I was winning awards frequently. There were no signs that I was crumbling inside. My family had no clue. My friends couldn't see it. I always had a remarkable story to tell about how wonderful things were going in my life. It was fun and exciting. I would throw fight parties when there was a big boxing match on Pay Per View. I was throwing Super Bowl parties with 40 to 50 people at my house. The life I was living was the one people envied. I had freedom. I had a great paying job. I was taking trips to Jamaica by myself. I was flying to Vegas and taking my son on trips to New York and California. I was living the dream.

It was during the writing of my first book that I realized that I had a problem with completing tasks. I had also enrolled in a PhD program to work on another degree and my youngest brother died suddenly. That caused everything in my world to come to a screeching halt. I dropped out of the PhD program and put my writing on hold. I became terribly angry with God. I questioned everything around me and my very existence. Of course, I poured myself another drink.

Not only did God take my brother away after making him suffer with uncontrollable diabetes, but we also found out that he had a tumor in his brain. We don't know if he died from the complications of the operation to remove the tumor (he died approximately two weeks later) or from complications of the diabetes. All I know is that my baby brother had only lived 25 years on this Earth. It was unfair. I ended up paying for his funeral but didn't get a chance to grieve. I was moving at the speed of lightning helping to plan the best homegoing service I could. That was a lot to carry. I drank heavily during this time. I remember how numb I felt at my brother's funeral, although I hadn't had any alcohol that morning. I sat in the front row in the church holding hands with my siblings. I stared at my brother's casket the entire time. I did not shed one single tear. I felt like I was made of steel. I was wearing big dark sunglasses. I had no interest in being there. I remember going to my parents' home afterwards and mingling with everyone. I hugged and kissed so many loving people. I thanked everyone who told me how "strong" I was. Meanwhile, I couldn't get to my hotel room fast enough to escape the wave of emotions that had been on my ass for the previous three weeks when all this started. I poured myself another drink.

I look back at that time in my life and I know I was burying my head in the sand, as opposed to speaking up and confronting issues and people who were affecting me. I turned the other cheek. I wanted to keep the peace and remain strong. I wanted to appear unbothered. That was the wrong thing to do because I ultimately internalized my feelings and only did more harm and damage to myself. My disease became worse. I was becoming an alcoholic.

Over the next few years, I would continue on the top performance path at work. I would continue to "live the dream," per se. I had people in my life who would ask to borrow money from me very often and it was becoming draining. I did not know how to say "no" to them. They could call me for anything, and I would be there to help them. I never understood that this was dysfunctional until I said "no" for the first time and they lashed out at me. It wasn't until then that I saw the dynamics for what they truly were. It hurt like hell. It was the wakeup call that I needed. I was shaken to reality that I was in this thing alone and I was going to have to stand up for myself if I was going to make it. No one was checking on me to see if I was okay or needed anything. No one really had my back. That felt lonely. At least the people closest to me in my immediate family were truly my rock. I had my siblings and my parents who I spoke to quite often. I'm happy to say that I also had the support of a few dear friends. Other than that, I came home every day to an empty home and the record of loneliness was on repeat. I started to feel the walls closing in on me. Guess what I did. You guessed right. I poured another drink.

I let the record play on for many years like this. Eight more years to be exact. Ten years after my divorce, I had not done the proper healing. I had not sought out the appropriate help to learn to cope with the stressors of my day-to-day life. Although my life appeared to be wonderful, I was barely hanging on by a thread. I finally decided that it was time to get help. This decision didn't come easily. It occurred to me one day when I was trying to put together a piece of office furniture and I kept getting frustrated. As I sat in the middle of my home office with pieces of furniture strewn all around me and little nuts, bolts, and screws in disarray, I realized that this was a picture of my life. I needed someone to come in and help me with the step-by-step directions. I needed someone to come in and help me pick up the pieces and put them together. That was the first time I called our company's Employee Assistance Program. I felt vulnerable and helpless.

The lady on the other end of the phone line was extremely kind. She was patient and her voice was calm yet concerned. She asked a series of questions that confirmed that I qualified for counseling services. In a matter of minutes, I was set up with an appointment with a therapist in my local community. My appointment was set for a few days later and I was eager to go in and get fixed. Little did I know there was still a small part of me that was not ready to face the bigger parts of me that were so broken, shattered, and wounded. I went in and filled out the extensive paperwork. I did not hold back. The question about how much alcohol do you consume per week? Yeah, I was honest about that, too. My therapist's name was Melissa. She was a hippie looking woman with long, brown, curly hair. She welcomed me with a warm smile. As she ushered me into her office, I took a seat on the plush couch across from her. I noticed a box of Kleenex on the table. I thought to myself, *"I hope I won't need that."*

Melissa was concerned about what brought me in to see her. She was aware that I was referred to her through my Employee Assistance Program (EAP), and she assured me that everything we talked about would be confidential. I shared with Melissa how I had been struggling to concentrate, not sleeping very much, and drinking loads of alcohol, which I felt made me feel better. Melissa shocked me. She told me that we needed to "throw the alcohol into the sea of forgetfulness" because it was making my symptoms of depression worse. I wanted to pack my things and immediately walk out. I wanted to throw Melissa into the sea of forgetfulness! How dare she suggest I get rid of the one thing that was providing comfort? I mentally checked out at that point.

I knew that this therapy thing wasn't for me. The irony is that I had worked for years as a therapist, having earned my master's degree in social work and my bachelor's degree in psychology. I knew exactly what I was doing. I was sabotaging my own healing process before it even began. I decided my first session with Melissa would be my final session. I could handle therapy on my own. I went to the liquor store and bought some vodka, went home poured myself a drink, and called one of my male playthings to come hang out.

I avoided therapy again for a number of years. It wasn't until 2016, that I admitted I was running on fumes and couldn't recognize myself anymore that I knew something had to give. My depression was back in full force, and it was affecting every area of my life. I was no longer taking care of myself. I was barely eating; and I was not sleeping at all. My manager and my coworkers noticed the changes. I was taking sick days like crazy. I could barely get out of bed in the mornings. My world was caving in around me. I would lay in bed and cry hysterically because I was afraid to tell anyone.

I was more so embarrassed about what I had become. I thought no one knew, but the day that I called my manager and broke down in tears because I was so overwhelmed, completely shocked me. She encouraged me to take a sick day and pull myself together.

I spent the morning lying in bed until I was stirred to my feet when the doorbell rang. My manager had sent a bouquet of fruit with a card that read, "Even the best of us just need a day off sometimes." She also noted how much she appreciated my work (I had been leading in sales in a large territory on my own for eight months). Her words meant so much to me. To see those words gave me the motivation that I needed to get up and get moving. I cleaned my home that day, did laundry, and organized my office. I felt important. I had gotten my second wind. I no longer felt invisible. I went to work the next day with a new attitude.

Not long after that episode, my energy began to wane again. My manager had hired a new partner for me who ended up quitting before she even got started. I was devastated. We had to go through the entire hiring process, again. I continued to hold down my territory on my own and make sure my customers had what they needed but once again, I was bone-tired. I was driving all over the place maintaining my key accounts and the pressure was on me to stay at the top. But I created that pressure. No one ever said to me, "Dana, you must maintain the number one spot." It was the perfectionist in me that wanted to prove to others that I, alone, could do the job, with or without a partner. I wanted to show myself worthy of selling. I wanted people to finally see my skills outside of the shadows of the partners that I had always had. Partners, whom I believe, stole the limelight simply because I was invisible. For as long as I was with that company, I was always the minority on the team; and always felt like I had to prove myself. Now, was my time to shine and boy, was I shining. But at a deadly cost to myself. It was all in my head, and no one knew the depths of the horrible rat race I had created for myself. Or did they?

My daily routine consisted of waking up after only two to three hours of sleep (I never slept more than three hours after my divorce). If my son were home, I would get dressed, take him to school, go to work, make sure I had enough vodka for my evening cocktail, go home and drink. My goal was to drink until I was finally sleepy but that never happened. So, I sat on my patio, listening to Pandora, smoking cigarettes, and drinking one vodka after another into the wee hours. I would sometimes get up at 4:30 a.m. and go to the gym by 5:00 a.m., but that was inconsistent since I was weak from not eating properly. I was a complete and utter mess. It's a miracle I was functioning.

I eventually took another sick day. I spent part of that day crying and feeling overwhelmed. I sent my girlfriends a group text which asked, "Do you ladies ever feel like giving up?" Thank God, they took me seriously because not long after that text message there was a knock at my door. One of my coworkers had come by to check on me. One look at the mess I was in, and she sat me down and said to me,

"Okay, we're calling the Employee Assistance Program right now. If you don't call them, I'm calling them."

Julie didn't leave me a choice that day. She sat by my side as I called the EAP and shared with the operator on the line how overwhelmed I was. It was immediately agreed that I needed to take a leave of absence to pull myself together and get help for my depression. I was terrified.

"What if I lose my job? I'm a single mom! I need my job! I can't depend on anyone else to take care of me or my son!"

The young lady on the phone assured me that my leave of absence would be confidential and that my job would not be in jeopardy. She set me up with a counselor for the next day and scheduled a time for me to see my doctor. I felt a sense of relief knowing that I was taking a step in the right direction, but I was horrified of what was awaiting me. I was used to my routine. My life had become so chaotic, but I was functioning in this comfortable chaos.

Once Julie confirmed that I had all my resources set, she hugged me and told me that she would check on me later. Not long after she left, Kate showed up at my front door. What the hell was this? My girlfriends were not taking that text message lightly and I'm thankful for them. Kate sat with me for hours and we chatted about life. Kate looked around my dark home and kindly suggested I change the color of my walls to brighten things up. Just the simple thought of changing my walls threw me into a fit of anxiety! Kate stayed with me into the evening hours. She had brought over something light and made sure I ate dinner and went on her way. This was a pivotal day in my journey because no matter how much my illness wanted me to believe that I was alone and that no one loved me, my friends came through for me and held down the fort.

I was able to go in for therapy the next day and I was nervous as hell. I ended up meeting with Melissa, the same therapist who attempted counseling me previously. Melissa was so welcoming. She didn't waste any time explaining to me what approach she was going to take in our second attempt at working together. She explained to me that since I was on a leave of absence, I needed to maximize my time and get the proper help I needed. She suggested a great treatment program that she was aware of and thought I would fit right in. Melissa went on to say, "You'll love it." I cussed her out in my head while smiling and nodding.

"I think this will be good for you. The group is made up of all kinds of people. People like yourself who are professionals seeking help for their mental illnesses and addictions. I'm so excited for you. I just sent a firefighter there that I've been working with and he's doing great. Oh! And there's a banker, yeah, she's doing great, too. Trust me, you'll meet people just like you."

That information made me even more nervous. All I wanted to know was if I was going to have to give up my alcohol. That was the irony in my concern – this program specifically focused on addictions. Oh, hell no! And she wanted me to agree to this on the spot. Melissa basically laid out my options for me and in my current situation, I didn't have many. I was either going to sink or swim. I knew that I had to do this. When she told me that it would only be a few hours Monday through Friday, I knew I had to give myself a chance. I agreed, Melissa made the phone call, and I attended my first group treatment meeting the next day. I was terrified, but Melissa assured me that she had also set me up with one of the best therapists in the facility, so I'd also begin to do individual work while attending the intensive outpatient group treatment program.

C H A P T E R   5

Round One of Treatment:

Yes, this chapter is titled Round One because, unfortunately, I would end up having to try that thing again (we'll get to that a little later). I was extremely nervous the morning I was headed to Breakthroughs to start my sober journey. Still, I made sure to drink my ass off the night before. I remember telling myself, "Welp! This is it!" I thought that would be the last time alcohol touched my lips and decided to enjoy all the libation I could joyfully. What a terrible miscalculation.

I arrived at Breakthroughs at 8:45 a.m. As I parked my car in front of the building my heart started pounding as if it were about to burst through my chest. I saw a small group of people standing off to the side in an area that I would soon become familiar with (the smoking section). They were laughing and talking, and EVERYONE was smoking or vaping. I got out of my car, took a deep breath, and headed to the entrance. As I was opening the door, a young girl dressed in goth came up to me.

"Hey, I'm Zola. First day, huh?"

I smiled at Zola and told her that I was so nervous about this decision. She reassured me that it was going to be the absolute best decision I would ever make in my life. All I could think was, I damn sho'll hope you're right. I had that sentiment because I was still in the trenches. I still had alcohol running through my veins. The interesting thing about facing the fact that I needed to stop drinking is that I didn't believe in my heart that I could do it. It seemed completely impossible and the thoughts I would have about living sober centered around the idea that I simply didn't know what I would do as an alternative to drinking. For eight long years, alcohol had soothed me in my worst moments. Alcohol gave me courage. It made me bold. It made me feel exhilarated and that felt good. I wanted to feel that feeling all the time, as much as I could. Little did I know God was up to something and He would eventually lead me to see that I was all those things without the alcohol, and better yet, I would be even more courageous and even more bold without the effects of alcohol blunting my true personality.

When I went inside the building. There was a door and a window to the right of the lobby. There was a window where I was to sign in. I approached the sign-in sheet, and, per the directions, I printed my first name and last initial only. I smiled at the woman behind the glass window as she cracked the window opened and told me to go ahead and take a seat in the group room which was the door to the left. My heart felt like it was trying to reset itself every 30 seconds. My breathing had picked up and I started to wonder if this is what a panic attack feels like. My palms were sweaty, and I kept thinking that this moment felt unreal. Doubts were racing through my head. Was I really doing this? I found my way over to the door and entered the room where major life changes were about to take place. Little did I know, I had chosen the right door……you know life is like a game show at times, you literally must hope and pray you've chosen the right door.

The group room was a large area with chairs set up in a circle to fill the entire space. There had to be at least 20 chairs. There was a blue book on each chair (that little book would be vital to my treatment and healing). The room smelled like fresh coffee, and I could hear the coffee machine percolating off to the right. There were probably 10 people seated in the room. People huddled here and there, and a few were seated in chairs, staring down at their cell phones. It was probably about four minutes to 9 a.m. I smiled to those who made eye contact as I made my way to the far side of the room. I chose a chair flanked by two empty chairs. As soon as I sat down, I looked up and a big husky White dude was staring at me from across the room. Before I could look away, he blurted out,

"First day, huh? You nervous? You gon' be alright!" I loved his Southern drawl.

I smiled and mouthed the words, "thank you," because suddenly, my voice was gone. Unexpectedly, I couldn't speak. My hands were shaking, my pulse was racing, and there was this overwhelming rush of emotions. The tears welled up in my eyes so surprisingly; I had no time to shield myself and hide from these strangers. The dam had broken. That one phrase, "you gon' be alright" sent me into a tailspin. It reaffirmed what I already knew to be true: I'm gon' be alright, but HOW and WHEN and at what cost?

The room quickly filled as I tried with all my might to pull my shit together. The reality of this new journey was setting in faster than I expected it to. People walked over and introduced themselves, patted me on the shoulder, handed me Kleenex. Each person had a piece of advice for me since it was my first day. Finally, a man walked in and the people in the room erupted with excitement. As if the room wasn't already bustling and loud enough, jokes were thrown around and laughter exploded all around. I eventually came to understand what had just happened because in a matter of weeks I was reacting the same way when Britt walked into the room!

Sometimes I look back over my life and I recognize specific times and places when my life was changed due to the influence of another person. It's so cool to sit and reflect sometimes and I often find myself saying "wow, okay, now I see the purpose in that relationship." Well, that's how I felt about Britt. He was one of the three group leaders at the time that I attended treatment. His story is so dynamic, and he exudes hope, change, and resilience. From the day I met Britt, I wanted to push harder toward my goal of being alcohol free. Britt had this consistent positive attitude and outlook on life. He shared his own personal struggles with addiction and his story was proof that it could be done.

As I consider that first day at group, it was Britt's kind and encouraging words that made me want to return the next day. The group was so non-threatening, and it was a safe space for me to talk through my issues with addiction and to learn better coping skills. So, the moment had finally arrived where I was supposed to utter those disgusting words while introducing myself to the group. As the greetings began, Britt started out by stating his name and his addiction, his sober date, and how long he'd been clean and sober. I was on the opposite side of the circle, so it took a minute to get to me. My heart pounded harder and faster with each introduction. I was in such a nervous tizzy that I didn't hear what the other group members were saying. Then, the spotlight was on me. Literally ALL eyes on me and I could feel the anticipation in the air. My lips wouldn't move. I could not bring myself to admit to these strangers my deepest darkest secret. I refused to say it aloud so instead I said,

"Hi, I'm Dana. As you all can see it's my first day, I'm super nervous, and to be honest, I don't want to be here."

To my surprise, the group began to clap in thunderous unison. Britt was clapping, too. I was a bit confused, and it showed on my face because once Britt got the crowd to calm down, he spoke directly to me:

"The reason we're clapping for you is because we've all been in that same seat that you're sitting in. We remember our first time coming to grips with our reality. You're in the right place and everyone in here will tell you that it's completely up to you how things turn out. All I can say is that the ball is in your court now. It's up to you to do the hard work to beat your addiction. No one can do that for you."

The entire time Britt was speaking, I was looking at my lap fighting back tears with every syllable. I wanted to melt into a puddle and evaporate. Everyone was staring at me, and I heard various voices chiming in as Britt drove home that being in that room meant business. Britt continued to break the ice by asking me open-ended questions. This allowed me to get a little more comfortable with speaking in front of those in the room. I shared how I was on a leave of absence from work and my therapist recommended this program to help me with my trouble with alcohol. Britt asked me what I did for a living, and I explained that I was in sales. That's when he pointed to Elizabeth, a few seats over from me.

"You should link up with Elizabeth! She's in Corporate America, too. She has shared a lot of her frustrations and how her job led to her heavy drinking. What do you think, Elizabeth? You cool with that?"

Elizabeth had a kind smile. She looked to be in my age bracket. She looked amazingly comfortable in a pair of cute yoga pants and a tank top. She wore flip flops that were on the floor because she had her feet tucked under her butt with her knees jutted out. She jumped into the discussion with excitement:

"ABSOLUTELY! I'm more than happy to help you! It's an interesting journey, for sure. I can help you with resources, anything! Just let me know!" Elizabeth was beaming!

I smiled at Elizabeth and nodded my head at Britt. "Thank you so much. I'm super nervous today because I just don't know if I can do this. I know that showing up was the first step, but now that I am here, all I can think about is going by the liquor store, going home, and sitting on my patio with my drink. The best part of my day. Or so I used to think."

Britt acknowledged what I said, then went on to explain how the group works to me and a couple of other newcomers. He explained that we were accountable for our own behavior, actions, and progress, and that Breakthroughs was there as a resource to us. We were expected to participate and contribute to our healing. A woman then walked into the room and excused herself before kneeling to whisper into Britt's ear. Britt looked up and yelled my name. I was a little startled. He told me that I needed to go with Petergay for my one-on-one therapy session. Petergay was standing at the door by now and signaled for me to follow her.

Petergay led me to a room right outside of the group room. It was very cozy with pastel colors on the walls and beautiful paintings. It was dimly lit with two floor lamps in opposite corners. There were two couches on either side of the room and there was a desk in the corner with two chairs on the opposite side. Petergay asked me to pick a place I liked. I chose the loveseat. As I sat down, I grabbed one of the throw pillows. It was plush, soft, and felt good in my arms. I held it close to my chest as I waited for Petergay to begin our session.

Petergay was a young Black woman. She was very pretty with natural hair styled in loose twists. She was dressed in a pair of black ankle pants and a royal blue blouse that draped in the front. She was humming softly to herself as she rearranged papers in a folder on her desk. She pulled one of the chairs in front of the desk in my direction, being mindful to respect my space. She then told me what her purpose would be and what her specific role would be in my treatment journey. She set a timer and placed it on a small table as she shared that our initial session was simply for us to get comfortable with one another and to pinpoint the specific goals that I would begin working on. I was less nervous by then. There was a light feeling. I felt almost excited. Though I couldn't really tell because things were still a bit foggy from my crazy alcohol binge the night before. All I knew was that I was going to have to take this opportunity seriously and get down in the dirt to find my healing. I had no idea of what would await me. The first step was to admit that I had a problem.

Petergay and I discussed the fact that I was having a hard time admitting my struggle with alcohol and I was trying every way possible to minimize the seriousness of this problem. I had every excuse as to why I drank alcohol the way that I did. I blamed my divorce, I was a victim, a single mother holding down a household on my own, I had a stressful job that requires me to end each day with loads of vodka, I was being used by people, etc. Whatever situation or challenge you could name, I'd find a reason to pour one up. Petergay encouraged me to be as honest as possible during our sessions so that we could really do the work. I would later come to appreciate that introduction the most because little did I know I was starting to uncover my truth. I would soon learn to accept everything about myself (good and bad), and I would start a bit of the movement to encourage others to Live in Truth. More on that a little later.

We spent the next 45 minutes walking through my childhood, my educational background, and the dynamics of my life then (my family structure, career, financial status, social life, etc.). We were setting the foundation. What would occur over the next six weeks was magic. After our time was up, Petergay advised that we should meet for an hour once per week. She wanted to address one more thing before we went back into the group room. She was concerned about my resistance to admitting aloud that I am an alcoholic. I explained that I had always had this image of an alcoholic ever since I was a little kid. An alcoholic was that dirty, raggedy clothes-wearing person walking down the street with a brown paper bag with alcohol of some sort inside. They were always drunk and staggering throughout the neighborhoods. They were poor and often homeless. They hung out in front of my Dad's Corner Grocery. They were sad and pathetic. They represented depression and doom. So, clearly, I was NOT an alcoholic. I had my shit together. Petergay burst my little bubble. We ended the conversation with this:

"Since you're not comfortable saying that you're an alcoholic, what do you prefer to say when you address the group and acknowledge your purpose for being in the group?" Petergay asked me with a perplexed look on her face.

"The way I see it, I am a woman seeking sobriety." I stated with confidence.

There was a long pause accompanied by a blank stare. Before we knew it, Petergay and I both were laughing hysterically. She told me that she was cool with that terminology, however, she still wanted to see me eventually get to that point where I would truly state my truth. My truth was that I had struggled with alcohol for eight years and I was no longer in control. I agreed to work hard to utter those words, "Hi, ……" Uuuuuugh! Some day.

When Petergay and I went back into the group room, it was 11:20 a.m. and the room was empty since break time had begun. Petergay told me she was going to get some things done and she encouraged me to go outside and mingle with the others. There were a few people huddled in different corners of the room, but I took her suggestion and went outside. It was such a beautiful sunny day. The sky was bright blue. I walked over to a bench where two women were sitting. They were smoking cigarettes. I decided to join them, so I pulled out my vape. I introduced myself again. That was the beginning of my sober sisterhood with Elizabeth and Lena. They were so welcoming and friendly. They also didn't hold back on sharing their stories with me. We exchanged phone numbers just as it was time to return to the group for the last 20 minutes.

Britt quieted us down as everyone piled back into the room. He looked over at me and asked me if I was doing okay. He also asked me if things went okay with Petergay. I told Britt that I was feeling hopeful. Britt then handed me a piece of paper as he explained, "Your first assignment, young lady. Take your time and complete this assignment by next Friday." He then walked over to other newcomers, sat down in his seat, and recapped the things that we discussed in the group earlier. He encouraged all of us to continue to do the work every second of every day. He went around the room and checked in with each person in that circle. It was so powerful to see how a simple gesture like asking, "you good?" to someone can make them feel seen. At the end of the day that's all we really want. We want to be seen, liked, loved. That's what keeps some of us alive sometimes. I felt that then. I felt safe surrounded by people who were just like me. No one looked dirty, poor, or homeless. This room was filled with people from all walks of life. Some were addicted to drugs, others struggled with sex, alcohol, shopping, gambling. We were all there to face our demons. We were all addicted to something that had affected our lives. When you become a part of a circle like that you can't help but want to strengthen the group by holding down your end of the bargain. You want to own your truth.

When it was time for the group to end, Britt stood up and everyone else in the room rose and joined hands in a circle. I looked around the circle taking it all in. This would be my second home for the next several weeks. What I didn't know while standing in that circle for the first time, hands interlocked with strangers, was that my entire life was about to change. Some of those faces would be there for a long time and then they would move on. Some would graduate from the program. Some would go on to live successful lives, some would return to the program multiple times before they got it right, and some would die. Yes, some did die.

As we held hands, Britt asked in an excited voice, "Who wants to start us off?" Hands shot up in the air, "Okay, Matt, take us on out of here," Britt encouraged.

In unison, the group recited the "Serenity Prayer". While I am familiar with it and could have joined them, I chose not to. I felt embarrassed and even though no one was paying me any attention, I still felt like everyone was staring at me. I looked down at my shoes and quietly thanked God it's a short prayer and I could soon bolt for the door:

> ***"God grant me the serenity to accept***
> ***the things that I cannot change,***
> ***The courage to change the things that I can,***
> ***And the wisdom to know the difference."***

After the prayer, everyone chanted loudly: "Keep coming back! It works if you work it!"

I felt this rush of excitement. I don't know if it was because I was proud of myself for making it through the first group and individual sessions or if I was simply eager to get back home. I was a little nervous about how my first night without alcohol was going to go. I had made up in my mind that I needed to be done with alcohol for the last time. It was a scary thought as I gathered my purse and coffee mug and headed for the door. Britt signaled for me to come over to where he was standing near the exit.

"So, how you feeling? I mean for real. You feel like you gonna be okay?" Britt asked, concerned.

"To be honest with you, I was just wondering how the rest of my day is going to go. I am not used to not drinking. I have no idea how I'm about to do this," I was visibly upset.

Britt pointed at one of the chairs in the circle and we walked over, and I sat down. Britt walked over to a set of shelves on the wall, grabbing a small stack of paper. He handed it to me and told me to get ready to stay busy.

"Here are some exercises that you can work on that will help you get stronger, and they will also help you learn how to cope with your emotions and feelings. You are about to feel things you haven't felt in a long time because the alcohol used to keep you numb. Even now, you're still adapting to your body not having alcohol. It's going to take time physically, mentally, emotionally, spiritually, all that. Trust me on this. Just do the work." Britt sounded so sincere. You could hear the yearning in his voice to save someone else. His life's work.

I thanked Britt for the work he had given me. We said our farewells and I headed out to my car. I sat in my car and let the air conditioner run for a minute. I turned my music down and took a deep breath. I knew that I was going to have to continually remind myself throughout the day that this is what is best for me. Now that I tackled the first challenge on the journey (attending group therapy), I fought back the urges that were rising up in me. It was only 12:30 p.m. and I had the rest of the day to myself. Any other time I had that much free time, I would be drinking my ass off and letting my problems slowly eat away at me. I was immediately stricken with fear. My heart started racing and my palms were sweaty. I was thinking too much, and I needed to get out of my head. I decided to call my best friend, my sister, Latricia. Thankfully, she answered right away. She was one of the few people who knew about the journey I was embarking on. My sister listened as I told her about my experience that morning in treatment. She was so supportive, and she kept telling me that she was so proud of me. Little did she know that gave me hope. More hope than I had felt in a long time. I talked to my sister the entire drive home because I was afraid that I'd stop at a liquor store. I made it home and decided to share my assignment with my sis. I shared that the assignment would be due the following Friday, then I read the instructions.

They were simple: "Write a farewell letter to alcohol. Be sure to express your feelings with regards to how alcohol made you feel, how alcohol affected your relationships, your job, your finances. Be sure to include your plan moving forward without alcohol."

My sister was ecstatic. Meanwhile, back at the ranch, I was terrified! Writing this letter meant that I was serious. I knew it had to be done. Safely in my house, I ended my phone call with my sister and got to work on the letter to alcohol. I felt like it was the first step to actually admitting to myself that I am an alcoholic. I sat for a long while at my dining room table with a pen and one of my journals. I started to pray softly. Before I knew it, God was moving through me, and I was writing this letter to alcohol. It felt as if God had taken the pen from my fingers and completely took over. What resulted was this letter which I read to the entire group that Friday.

Dear Alcohol,

I am writing to you to inform you that our relationship has run its course, and I am no longer available to hang out. I wanted so much to keep my words kind and gentle, as I always am when confronting a sensitive subject, but this calls for me to take the mask off (and the gloves, too). I have grown to hate you. I used to love our daily meetings and social time together. You had a way of making me feel so good. Then I started to notice how possessive you became. It was never enough to have just one. It became imperative that you consume every ounce of my being. You wanted to be the center of my life and I welcomed you in.

I would wake up with you on my mind. I would push through my workday just to get back home to you. And then you put me to sleep at night. Well, the funny thing is all along, I knew you were trying to destroy me. I knew there was always an ulterior motive and to that I'm saying goodbye. I no longer desire the numbness you provided. I do not prefer dried-up tears. It's time to let my tears flow freely. It's time to release and it's time to FEEL. It's time to HEAL. You have served your purpose in my life and now it's time for you to go.

You taught me something. I do not love you. I despise you for what you've done, not just to me but so many people that I love. I have witnessed you destroy lives. You're so good at what you do. You're like a charming man that walks into a room with an agenda tucked under his coat (an agenda to hurt, harm, and destroy). You'll obviously stop at nothing.

I am here to say that I am done with you. No longer will I focus on you as if my life depended on it because now, I see more than ever before that I cannot survive if I keep you in my life. Surely, I will die. I have decided to live, and I've decided to fight. For the first time in 8 years, I can see clearly and I'm allowing myself to finally feel the hurt that I ran from. It was too painful to look at before. Now, I must face the consequences of having run away. I'm ready. I am equipped with the right tools, and I have people cheering for

me to win this battle. Once and for all, I am saying goodbye, Alcohol. Your work here is done. (February 2016).

I continued to attend group therapy and individual therapy for the next eight weeks. I did all the assignments, was a consistent participant in group therapy, and I was also making strides in my individual sessions. Petergay held my feet to the fire each week and for one hour I would dig through the baggage in my life that was no longer serving a purpose. I was able to walk through the history of my addiction. How it all started and why it all started, to get to the root of the problems. That was necessary to heal. Where does alcoholism stem from? For me it had everything to do with my perfectionism. I had so many beliefs about what life means and I was holding myself to an unreasonably high standard. I didn't allow room for mistakes. Through individual therapy, I learned that I was causing a lot of my own hurt and pain over the years because I was living my life according to a code that was unrealistic and completely unattainable.

Another requirement for completion of the treatment program was that I had to find an Alcoholics Anonymous (AA) meeting and participate. I chose to attend the AA meetings right after my session at Breakthroughs on Wednesdays at 12 o'clock p.m. I settled on that group because over weeks, I had attempted to find the right AA group for me, and I had failed miserably. There was one AA meeting less than four miles from my house located at the local University Alumni Hall, but that was a nightmare.

The first time I attended an AA meeting was during the second week of my treatment. When I first started my outpatient treatment program, I was given a booklet with what seemed like a million listings of local AA meetings with days and times, as well as locations. The meeting closest to my home (mentioned above) started that Wednesday evening at 6 p.m. and I arrived about 15 minutes early. There were older White men sitting and standing near the entrance to the hall, which was in the center of the campus. I greeted the group and made my way to the front door. Once inside, I was greeted by the beautiful smell of fresh brewing coffee. The room was large. It was clean and appeared to be a small theater with a stage up front and tables and chairs arranged neatly and uniformly throughout the room.

There were several people seated around what looked like a total of six long tables arranged in the shape of the letter U. I smiled at those who smiled at me as I found my way to the back of the room at one end of a table. I sat between two empty seats. I waited patiently as more people filed into the room. Some took the time to introduce themselves. That's one thing I can say about the AA community: you are going to feel welcome, no matter what your situation.

There were copies of the Big Book in front of every seat at the table. As soon as the clock struck 6:00 p.m., an older White man stood up at the head of the long tables. Let's call him Randy. Randy opened the group by introducing himself; he shared that he is an addict who has been sober for 23 years, and he's been leading this group for several years. He went over the rules of the AA meeting, and we began reading passages from the Big Book. We literally went all the way around the table with each member reading a sentence or two. Then it was time to share, and that is when I checked out. The rest of our time was spent with people sharing their journey and reminiscing about their past lives. It almost felt that most of them were in a living hell, longing for those days when life was one big party. The way so many of them spoke on how "sad" their lives are without alcohol, made me quickly lose interest. I knew that I couldn't be surrounded by that type of dialogue. I am extremely positive and forward thinking, so that type of energy was not for me. I also felt a lack of connection. I was the only Black person in the room, and this started to bother me throughout my treatment. Even in my treatment group at Breakthroughs, I was one of three Black people out of 25-30 people each day. At any rate, I did not give up after my first attempt at AA. I found another group at the beach specifically for professional women. I visited that location three times, but it still felt like I was surrounded by negative and sad energy. I understand that it comes with the territory because we're all dealing with an actual illness. There is no timeline for healing of any kind, so I respect that many were still feeling a major loss and life change. I simply could not get through the third time I visited the women's group. I told myself there is no way I'm going to go through this life missing alcohol. I was not going to be miserable. I decided that group was not for me, and I tried my hand at one last group that a friend told me about, but the same concerns existed there too. I was thankful that Breakthroughs offered AA. I felt comfortable because most of the people attending were also in the treatment group. The atmosphere was positive and there was less dwelling on the past. The group felt right for me.

As time went on, I began to fly solo, away from the support of my AA friends. I am in no way taking anything away from AA. It is an amazing resource. I found that speaking up about my first-hand experience with AA opened the door for other people to share their true thoughts. I think that when people think of "getting sober" they think of rehabilitation facilities, treatment programs, and a lifetime AA commitment. These things vary from person to person. The person who is struggling with alcohol must first decide that they need and want help. I can see the value in attending AA meetings, however, it's simply not for me. I'm also thankful to have survived, sober, thus far; and I plan to keep going.

C H A P T E R   6

Relapse & Rock Bottom

This inability to find the right AA meeting was pivotal in what would happen next for me. See, here's the thing. I thought for sure I had done all the work that I needed to do, and I felt like I had the right routines in place. My eating and my diet were well balanced, I was exercising at least 30 minutes per day, and I was avoiding environments that were unhealthy and triggering for me. I had dropped friends who didn't quite understand my newfound sobriety. I didn't realize how hanging out with certain people while new to my sobriety could eventually cost me everything. At around 10 weeks sober, I found myself out at dinner with some girlfriends. I must admit that by this time, I had convinced myself that I was healed and strong enough to avoid temptation. Little did I know, I should have stayed plugged into my resources.

The night was May 17, 2016, and I was out at a fancy restaurant with three girlfriends. The night was so amazingly fun. I couldn't believe how much self-control I exhibited as their various martinis and different flavored wines flowed to the table. I focused my attention on whatever funny topic we were discussing. I was laughing and enjoying myself without alcohol. I was doing fine. It wasn't until it was time to wrap things up and go our separate ways that an idea occurred. One of my friends kept insisting on stopping by my home so that she could see my kitten, Maddie

55

Merlot. She kept going on and on about how it had been months since she'd seen Maddie. So, I thought to myself, *"I actually have one last bottle of wine, maybe I can pop that open for her while she visits with Maddie Merlot."* And that was all she wrote.

When we arrived at my house, I got the wine opener and a bottle of wine. My friend cautioned me: "You really don't have to do that."

I insisted that it would help me "get this wine out my house." I got one whiff of that Merlot, and instead of pouring one glass for my friend, I ended up pouring myself a glass, too. We sat on my patio laughing and talking for over an hour and I felt exhilarated. I surmised in that moment that sobriety was stupid, and it made no sense at all to ever live without alcohol. I decided that I would simply exhibit more self-control and I wouldn't let alcohol control me. Fourteen days later, I hit rock bottom and found myself waking up in the hospital facing a new reality.

I decided on that night of my relapse that I'd never give up alcohol again. I decided I would moderate my drinking and limit the number of nights per week I drank. Initially, I told myself that I would only drink on the weekends. Obviously, that didn't work. I had zero self-control when it came to my drinking and as much as I strived to drink like a normal person, I simply couldn't stop at one. Over those 14 days, I tried hard to balance my work responsibilities. My counterpart at the time started questioning my wellbeing. While she was performing her duties as my partner, I was barely holding up my end. I was trying to portray organization yet sticking to my responsibilities throughout the day became increasingly difficult. It became painful. I had started the cycle again: drinking all night and dragging myself through the day, just to get back to my appointment on my patio with alcohol at night. I became more frustrated with myself because it was quickly becoming clear that I was losing this battle. Deep down, I was embarrassed, and I didn't know how to ask for help. I knew what I was doing was detrimental, however, I had too much pride to let my close family and friends know what I was going through. I even stopped communicating with Elizabeth from group therapy. I literally moved on and left my resources and coping skills behind.

Two weeks after my relapse, I got an impromptu phone call and invitation from my manager. She asked to meet in person because she had things she wanted to discuss with me. I already knew what the meeting was going to be about. I was not myself and I knew I had been made. When I arrived at the coffee shop at 10 a.m. on that Thursday morning, my manager greeted me with a hug. We ordered our coffee, found a table in the back corner, and she began.

"So, how have you been holding up? I'm a little concerned that you may have come back from your leave of absence too soon."

I was flabbergasted! I didn't have any words because I was caught off guard. The sad reality was that she was right, and it was at that moment that I broke, and I let the flood gates open. The tears streamed down my face quicker than I could wipe them away. I was mortified to be crying in a fucking coffee shop at 10 a.m. on a Thursday….IN FRONT OF MY BOSS! I let the tears flow; but I was careful not to share the details of my struggle with alcoholism because I was fearful of losing my job. The good thing about the EAP and taking a leave of absence is that everything is confidential. I was thankful for that because I didn't want anyone to know.

Through my tears, I was able to tell my manager that I felt like I was going to be okay; but coming back to work had its challenges. We discussed ways that I could get a better grip on my territory. I shared with her that I was going to put forth a better effort. I had a meeting set up with my partner for later in the day and I had every intention of strategizing with her to come up with a better game plan. Well, it was during that meeting with my partner that she shared with me that she had spoken with our manager about me. I felt blindsided. That explained my manager's concerns. I was angry and told her that I wished she had spoken to me first about her concerns. Now that I am clearheaded, I can look back on that situation and see it differently. My counterpart was only doing her job. But it's the anger and humiliation that I felt in that moment that would send me over a cliff.

Being a perfectionist all my life, I quite often found myself in uncomfortable positions. It was so important for me to be liked and loved so when I was confronted by both women about my professional slips, it brought back awful feelings of how it feels to be rejected. It also reminded me that there's nothing you can do to make others like you. Why did I care so much? That drove me insane because on the one hand, I remember what it felt like to be confident. I was fighting my way back to that feeling, but right now, alcohol was winning again.

I drank my ass off that night. I remember my mind was racing a million miles per minute. In my drunken rage, I recall playing hard-core rap music, calling any of my friends on the phone who would listen to me rant about how my partner threw me under the bus. I was beyond pissed, and I was planning to act. I was out of my mind.

The next morning was Friday. I had stayed up all night drinking and I felt like my world was spinning out of control. I had just enough strength to text my manager and tell her that I needed to take a sick day. Thankfully, Taz was with his dad, and I didn't have to worry about getting him until later in the afternoon after school. I was disappointed with myself. That was not uncommon. There's a lot of guilt associated with addictions. I kept replaying the meetings and conversations I had the day before with my manager and counterpart. The sickness of depression had me believing they were trying to ambush me and threaten my job. I felt like I needed to defend myself. Then something occurred to me. There was a sliver of hope or positivity left deep down within me because I recalled what my manager had addressed in terms of me possibly having returned to work too soon.

She had no clue as to why I was struggling, and by law, there was no way for her to find out. I was feeling anxious, and I also felt hopeless. Despite those feelings, something told me to pick up the phone. Minutes later I was sitting in my dining room crying on the phone with a counselor from the EAP - again. I felt so much shame – again. The counselor consoled me and reassured me that I was doing the right thing. I told her that I was afraid, and I didn't think I was going to make it. During that phone call, the counselor was able to reach out to Breakthroughs where I had received treatment during my first attempt at sobriety. She told me that I was all set to start back in the group therapy/outpatient program and I could start on Tuesday since Monday was Memorial Day. I felt so relieved. She shared with me that I would be approved to take another leave of absence and my job would not be affected. She told me that the main priority was to get me sober so that I could start doing the hard work again. Although I felt better knowing that I was going to start treatment again, the sick mind that I was operating from convinced me that I should live it up and truly get this desire out of my system before Tuesday. I was going to get it all in before I took the plunge into the Sea of Sobriety for good. That was the worse game plan EVER.

Once I realized I'd be off for a while to address this serious issue in my life, I felt more at ease. For the remainder of the morning and early afternoon, I lay in bed exhausted from the race I had been running. My body felt beat down and my brain was mushy. I had little strength left to keep pretending and it was bubbling over. I had been backed into a corner and with the little bit of ability I had left to be rational, I spoke to myself. I told myself that I must get a grip on my life. The fear was debilitating. The one glimmer of hope on that Friday was that I was going to pick my son up from school and I had planned to do pizza and a movie at home with him. I was in and out of hope on days like this. It was a constant battle. I struggled all the time with recognizing that I was not putting my best foot forward in the parenting department. Just as I had been doing with my career, I was faking the funk when it came to parenting, as well. It's a hard truth, but it is my truth. Let's just say I was doing the bare minimum and enough to survive in every area of my life. On the good days, I poured into my son as if nurturing him rushed from a fire hydrant! On the tough days, I sat in a blur at Taekwondo practices and competitions. I stared off into space at football games behind my dark sunglasses further hiding my truth. I was present in my son's life, but it was a struggle that took every ounce of my strength at times. I'm thankful that my clock did not run out on motherhood and what it meant to be Taz's mom.

That Friday afternoon, I followed through on my plan and picked my son up from school. We swung by our favorite pizza place at the beach and made our way home. I must admit, I was feeling extremely depressed and anxious, but I tapped into the energy my son provided at the time. Unfortunately, I was zoned out during our movie time because all I could think about was checking out with my favorite vodka drink. When my son went to bed that night, the chaos began. Over the next 72 hours, my life would take the most drastic turn.

I drank all night well into Saturday morning. I probably slept for a couple of hours, but all I can recall is waking up and fixing a drink at 9:30 a.m. I called my older sister around 10 a.m. and she knew something was wrong. I was ranting and raving about my job and how my manager and partner were ganging up on me. She worked hard to calm me down. Somehow, I convinced her that I was fine, and I hung up the phone. Little did I know, my sister called my son's cell phone and told him to call my ex-husband. She knew something was terribly wrong. During that time while I was out on my patio drinking alcohol and smoking cigarettes at 11 a.m., my mom called. She was frantic at the news my sister had shared with her about my drunken stupor at 10 a.m. on a Saturday morning. I will never forget that phone call.

In all my fog, and in all the haze, I heard my mother crying and begging me not to hurt myself. I kept telling my mom that I was "tired." I told her over and over that I was "done." It still breaks my heart when I reflect on that conversation. She was helpless and miles away. And I was determined to end it all. I apologized to my mother and hung up the phone. What happened next almost knocked me off my feet. I looked up through my dazed, confused state, and saw my ex-husband stepping out onto my patio. I flipped out! "What the FUCK are you doing here?"

Apparently, when my sister reached out to my son, she was able to speak to my ex-husband and she asked him to check on me. I was livid. I directed it all toward my ex. I cussed him out from A to Z. It was as if I was releasing every single ounce of hurt and pain that he had inflicted on me over the years. I had flashbacks to the first six months of our relationship when he lied straight to my face. We went to freaking couples counseling within the first year of our relationship because my university offered free services. What was I thinking ignoring all those red flags in the beginning? We were in counseling because he cheated back then, we were in counseling during our short-lived marriage because he cheated, and now the idea of him standing on my patio trying to help me pissed me off even more. I blamed him for all of it! I was screaming at him at the top of my lungs. He had taken a chair from the patio table and turned it toward me; he sat and let me strike him over and over with the words, "I HATE you!!!" I lashed out. I cried. I moaned. The hurt of it all felt just as painful coming out as it had felt going in, but something magical was happening. In the ugly thick of it all, I was being transformed.

Not long after my ex arrived, his mother also arrived. I flew into another rage. I was so humiliated, and I begged them to leave me alone. They saw the mound of old cigarette butts in my make-shift ash tray (an old candle jar). They saw the alcohol in my 20-ounce tumbler. My hair was a mess. I looked awful. I felt like I was being judged. The looks on their faces showed pity and surprise. My mother-in-law tried to console me. She was holding my hand and telling me we needed to go inside the house. While she was coaxing me inside, I had no clue that my ex-husband was inside with my son going through my medicine cabinet and pouring out all the alcohol beneath the kitchen sink. I would later find out that my ex was trying to see if one of the medications was causing the melt down.

When they finally got me inside, my Uncle James (dad's youngest brother to whom I am super close) arrived. He is the only family I have in Jacksonville (where I live), so my parents had called him to check on me, as well. As if that wasn't enough people there to witness my downfall, my ex-sister-in-law showed up, too. By then, they had me sipping coffee and everyone was gathered around me in the kitchen and living room area. I had an audience and, boy, did they get an ear full. I told story after story about all the crazy things that were going on with work. I was exaggerating and blowing things out of proportion. In all my distortion, I knew deep down that I needed to own my shit. But at the time, the alcohol made me feel invincible. I was blaming everyone and everything around me. I couldn't face my reality on that chaotic Saturday. I was surrounded by people who loved me, and I eventually sobered up enough so that they felt comfortable enough to leave. I had heard a million different speeches that day. I was over it.

I didn't drink that night. That evening and night were uneventful except for one horrible incident. After everyone had left, I lit into my son. I don't recall all the words I said, but I verbally attacked him for calling his dad and I blamed him for everyone finding out about my problem with alcohol. Although I don't remember the exact words, my son still remembers. He turned 13 that year. In my recovery, we were able to talk about things and he shed tears as he told me I gutted him with the words I said to him that day. It shed light on the healing that had to take place between the two of us. I'm so thankful I have a forgiving son.

My parents decided to visit the next day. I had time to clean my home and prepare for their arrival after my mom had called early that morning to tell me she and my father were on the way. I couldn't help but think of the irony in this situation. I was 19 years old the first time I got drunk. I was attending college at Florida State University. I was living off campus with a roommate who decided to surprise me on my birthday with a bunch of booze and all her friends. I drank shot after shot of a strong cinnamon flavored liquor, Aftershock. The smell of it today makes me want to vomit. What I remember about how alcohol made me feel was the after-effect.

During my drunken phase, I recall being extremely flirtatious. I loved the newfound exhilaration and feeling free. I introduced myself to alcohol and whispered, "I'll be back soon." That next day was my birthday and my mother called to tell me she and my dad were on their way to visit. Who would have guessed that my first encounter with alcohol would eventually lead right to one of my final encounters with alcohol and my parents were there during both pivotal times. The first incident was when I was in college and hung over the morning of my 19th birthday. My mother walked me through how to make a hot pot of grits over the phone. It was hot alright (a hot mess). I told my mom I needed to shower and rest until they got there. Four hours later my parents were looking around my trashed living room. It was obvious what had taken place here. My parents took me out to lunch and made sure I had a good hearty meal. I couldn't stomach much, but it was exactly what I needed. Now, here we were all these years later and my parents were taking me out to eat again. This time my son was with us, and we took a walk on the beach. The beach has always been my favorite place on Earth, and it made sense to spend time there. The sun was shining, the sky was blue and clear, and I was surrounded by love. However, there was a storm brewing inside of me and as much as I pretended to be on the mend from the events from the day before, I was slowly fading away from reality.

My dad poured into me every second that he got with me. Those were the moments when my son was in lockstep with my mom a few feet ahead. My dad kept reiterating how important it is for me to never drink alone. He had no idea that's how I preferred it. But I nodded and agreed with everything that he said. I remember telling my dad that when I drank alone, it was to have time with my thoughts. In retrospect, I realize that my dad had a major point because it was my thoughts that eventually overpowered me.

My mom pulled me aside and shared every ounce of her own personal experience and hardships with alcohol. She shared that one day she looked in the mirror in disgust and told herself that she HAD TO STOP. I really wish it had been that simple for me. In that moment, my mom allowed me to express my fears and inner struggles. Yet, she was able to instill a glimmer of hope in me with every doubt that I released. The love I felt from my parents that day was beautiful, however, there was the dread of my reality that lingered and awaited my return. This caused severe anxiety within me.

I related to my mom when she shared that pivotal moment that she had experienced in front of her mirror. I had stood in front of my mirror a million-gazillion times. The alcohol was more powerful. It was such a horrible cycle of not wanting to feel and then trying to force myself to literally face my shit straight in the eyes. Alcohol always called for me and reminded me that I didn't have to put myself through the pain of actual living and feeling this shit. I could be dulled and numbed and not feel a thing. And that felt better. Sometimes not feeling is the best feeling in the world. These were the thoughts that were swirling through my head. Little did I know, while my parents were visiting me and had run to my rescue, I was subconsciously longing for a final escape.

My parents left the next day, which was Memorial Day. What I remember most about them leaving, was the moment they pulled out of my driveway and the overwhelming desire to run down the street to the liquor store and get myself a drink. Sadly enough, that's exactly what I did. I told Taz I would be right back. I hopped in my car and drove to the store like I was on autopilot. My mind was telling me to push through this and not drink; my body was physically craving alcohol. I was extremely anxious, my hands were shaking, and that little tingle on the right side of my neck and shoulders (my sign that it was time for a drink), was in overdrive. As I drove to the store, I felt waves of guilt thrashing over my body. I felt disconcerted. I hadn't even purchased the alcohol yet. I had every opportunity to turn my car around, but the thought of what would come after that first sip propelled me to get there quicker. I completely blocked out everything my family had poured into me over the prior weekend and recent days.

I remember this awful feeling as I pulled into my garage after my emergency alcohol run. I knew that I had to hide the alcohol or else Taz would see it and probably fall apart. Even in that moment, I was trying to hide who I was from my son. I stuffed the extra-large bottle of Merlot into my large purse. I was under the impression that if I drank wine instead of vodka tonight, that would help me control things better. It's amazing how the brain works to manipulate our own thoughts. I was talking myself into this drink fest versus talking myself out of it. I had been equipped with the tools I needed while in treatment at Breakthroughs and I abandoned them. I had received words of encouragement from my family and friends over the three days, but I completely blocked them out. I walked into the house with my stash of Merlot. Thankfully, Taz was in his room with his door closed so I made a beeline for my closet. I closed the door to my walk-in closet and found a beach bag hanging on the back of the closet door. I shoved the wine inside. I went into the kitchen, quietly opened the drawer where the wine opener was kept, grabbed a big ass cup out of the cabinet and headed back into my closet to start the process. I ended up not giving a shit if Taz found out, because by the end of the night, I was back out on my patio smoking, drinking, and blaring my music. Taz had gone to bed early that night and we didn't talk much. I was feeling so enraged with everything that had transpired. I knew deep down it wasn't my son's fault, so the guilt was gripping me. I sat there and let my thoughts wander. Finally in the wee hours of the morning I crawled into my bed and drifted off into oblivion.

CHAPTER 7

Life Changing Event

What happened on that next morning would absolutely change my and my son's life and affect everyone who loved me. After drinking all night, I had to peel myself out of bed to make sure Taz was taken to school. The thought of that suffocated me. I wanted to lay there under the cover forever. Something else started to happen as I brushed my teeth staring into the mirror. I looked like a person who had been hit by a Mack Truck. I got dressed and checked on Taz. He was all set for school. We stood in the kitchen and held hands just like any other morning, but that time Taz prayed a special prayer for me. Something about my prayer was off. I didn't say much, instead I kind of thanked God for our blessings and kept it moving. As we drove to Taz's school, gospel artist Travis Greene's song "Just Want You" blared through the car speakers. That alone was proof that I truly did want to be rescued. I had been playing the song on repeat for months. Its message talks about not wanting anything else except God. My favorite lines from the lyrics say:

"Take everything. I don't want it. I
don't need it, God. I just want you."

It wouldn't be until years later that I would realize the impact this song had on me. It was essential in my healing process. It was that song and those words that gave me hope that God could truly save me. I cried almost every morning in the shower listening to it. I prayed so hard during those times when my addiction was at its worst. As I drove Taz to school that morning, my mind was on those lyrics again. There was a storm brewing inside of me and I had these intensely overpowering thoughts. I reflected on the night before – hiding my alcohol in my closet and sneaking around my son. I felt this huge tug in my heart. I kept asking myself – "so, is this really how you're gonna live now?" The thought of the possible response crushed me. I had become that person. A full-fledged alcoholic. How did the "First EVER Miss Black Teen Lake Wales" and "Homecoming Queen" turn into this? I didn't recognize myself anymore and I hated what I saw in the mirror. I had convinced myself that I was dirty and unworthy of love. I had been pretending to be a boss when really, I was so, so broken. I admitted to myself that I was weak. I could no longer control my drinking, plus my eating and sleep were out of order, and my body was unfamiliar to me. The men that I let touch me were only satisfying a temporary itch. I hated who I had become.

Taz was quiet along our route. He was busying himself on his cell phone when we pulled up to the middle school. Taz told me he loved me as he got out of the car. I stared at my son, then I finally said, "I love you, too, Baby. Make good choices today."

As Taz walked away, I sat there for a long time. Just watching my baby enter his school building, knowing I'd never see him again. That was the most jarring thought, but somewhere in my thoughts, I had decided within myself that I didn't want to be that person. I wasn't going to live my life sneaking swigs of alcohol in my closet. I was convinced addiction was going to win. I knew I could never live without drinking my ass off every single day. I needed alcohol in my life, but since I could no longer drink like a normal person, I didn't see the point of being alive anymore. I don't know the exact moment I decided that day was the day. Through our healing process later on, Taz shared that he noticed I sat in front of his school for quite some time the morning of my decision and wondered why I hadn't driven off yet. I had never sat there and watched my middle schooler enter the building. I typically flew off into traffic before his little ass could get out of the car good. He told me that it hit a nerve with him, but he tried not to think too deep into it. He knew something was terribly wrong. That was the beginning of the end.

When I drove off, I remember thinking I needed more wine. I drank that entire huge bottle the night before. I started to picture my medicine cabinet. I was trying to visualize what types of pills I had. Unfortunately, that was not the first time I had thought of suicide and played this little "I wonder how many pills it would take?" and "I wonder if I have enough pills?" sick game in my mind. Over the years, I had many thoughts of suicide. The closest I ever got was while I was still married and having issues with my ex. I would always wonder what the easiest way was to end my own life. I had no desire to harm myself physically. See the irony in that? That's what I was telling myself, as if any form of suicide is less harmless or any less severe. Death is death and if you take your own life, you've caused yourself the ultimate harm.

My brain was still swimming in alcohol from the night before, so I was not thinking rationally at all. I really wanted to take some pills and drift off into nothingness. I didn't want these senses any longer (no desire to touch or be touched, no desire to smell, to taste, to see, and no desire to hear). I had chosen my exit and that required me to stop at the gas station, which was the only place I could find alcohol at 7 a.m. After I stopped, I spoke with one of my dearest cousins, who called to check on me. He was following up with me after the previous weekend was such a debacle. News travels fast in my family. The one pivotal thing I remember about our conversation was that I was not making a lot of sense. I was talking about how I was so tired. I was tired of trying. I was simply tired. Just as all my family had done over the weekend, my cousin asked what I needed to make things better. He also tried to convince me to drive home and sleep it off. Bless his heart. He tried with all his might to encourage me and keep me on the phone. Once I reached the gas station, I told him that I loved him, and I had to go.

The next words I said to him I will never forget. "So, guess what! Today's finally the day!" and then I hung up the phone.

As I drove home in my haze, I thought about how I could push myself to go to group therapy at Breakthroughs, since I had been reenrolled and was scheduled to restart that day. My depression won. I accepted, on that drive home, that my affair with alcohol was it for me.

When I arrived home, with my bottle of Merlot in hand, the first thing I did was pour myself a glass. I started cleaning my house profusely. I was scrubbing, rearranging, organizing, all while taking big sips of my wine. Meanwhile, it was not even 9 a.m. Once I started to feel a little buzzed, the thoughts really started rolling in. It was an ambush of negative, painful, debilitating thoughts about myself as a mother, my inability to perform at work, the realization that I hadn't been in a serious committed relationship since my divorce and what this meant was that I was incapable of being loved and no one wanted me. I disgusted myself and I was convinced there was no hope in the love and romance department. The embarrassment of hiding my addiction, the secrets I had buried inside. It was all excruciating.

Amid the bombarding thoughts I managed to write a letter to my ex-husband and my son. I would love to say that this was the most agonizing and heart wrenching thing I've ever had to do. However, depression has a way of contorting every inch of your brain and certain thoughts and behaviors simply do not make sense. Instead of the act of writing this letter snapping me back to reality, it was another sign of how ill I was. I felt that first sense of relief. I knew that once I wrote that letter and put the key out front under the welcome mat, it was game time. I won't share all the details of what I said to my ex and my son, but I will say this – I begged for him to love Taz for me. I begged him to let my son know that I was so sorry that I wasn't strong enough. I asked him to explain that I needed my rest, and they were both better off with me out of the picture. My hands were shaking horribly as I was writing. I was in the kitchen at the counter. I was bent over urgently pleading my case for what I thought was the last time. I didn't fold the letter or put it into an envelope. I simply left it face up on the kitchen counter.

By then, I was inebriated. I was no longer in control of my thoughts, but the house was clean, the letter had been written, and now it was time for me to take my rest. I went into my restroom and opened the medicine cabinet. Oddly enough, that was the calm part. I didn't hesitate when I grabbed the bottle of sleeping pills that hadn't been opened yet. I stood in front of the mirror and slowly began the process. I thought I'd feel instant regret, but surprisingly, once I took that first handful of pills, it's as if the motor started running. I was revved up and couldn't wait to check the fuck out! That's what moved me to pop those pills as fast as possible. It was as if I got excited about what was to happen next. In my mind, I imagined drifting off into a peaceful sleep and I'd never have to face this bullshit we call life. Ever again.

After I took the pills, I decided to go to my favorite spot in my home - my screened in patio. As you know (from reading my words thus far), I spent hours on that patio drinking, smoking, partying with family and friends. It was where I wanted to be when I drifted off for good. I knew that I should at least let my ex-husband know where I left the key for him to be able to get in and get Taz's belongings and our cat, Maddie Merlot. I hesitated when I reached for my phone because by then everything was spinning. I wanted to make sure I would be completely gone just in case he would try to talk me out of it or even save me. I was lucid enough to know I shouldn't talk. I don't think I could talk. I sent my ex the following text:

"Hey, I just wanted to let you know that I am done. I left the key under the mat so you can come in and get Taz's things."

My ex responded immediately: "Dana, are you serious? What are you talking about?"

After that text I closed my eyes and I started to drift off. I was shaken and startled after what felt like only a few minutes by my mother-in-law. I would later find out that my ex called her to rush over to my house since he couldn't get to my side of town as quickly. While that was happening, my ex was on the phone with my sister, and they decided to call 911. What I remember, in bits and pieces, is being shaken several times and talking to my sister-in-law who had been called by my mother-in-law. I wasn't holding the phone, but somehow my sister-in-law, who's a nurse, was speaking softly into my ear trying to find out what I had taken. I think I may have mentioned in previous text messages to my ex that I was going to take something. That is what likely made him take me seriously and call for reinforcements. Plus, it was only a few days earlier that these same characters were in the first dramatic scene when I got drunk and was subconsciously on the verge of suicide. No one who had come to my rescue that Saturday before had any way of knowing how sick I was. They had no way of knowing I would take the first opportunity when I was alone and try to end my life.

By the time the ambulance arrived at my house I was unconscious. I have no recollection of being taken out of my home on a gurney to a nearby urgent care hospital; or being sent to a larger hospital downtown once my condition was noted. I would wake up more than eight hours later in the hospital.

Coming out of my stupor, the first thing I thought was, "you have GOT to be FUCKING kidding me!" I had all sorts of tubes coming out of my arms and as my vision cleared, I saw my uncle and aunt standing over me. They immediately started to comfort me, and they worked hard to calm me down. I was crying hysterically. I remember feeling waves of guilt pounding over me. I felt like I was drowning. It hit me in a matter of seconds how big this moment was. Not only had I attempted suicide and failed miserably, but now I had to live in this reality. The reality where everyone now knows how deep my secret ran. Everyone knows my SECRET. FUCK!!!!!!

Over and over, I kept saying, "I'm soooooooo sorry. I'm soooooooo sorry. I'm so sorrrrrry."

I could not stop crying. I felt awful and I was still a little woozy. I asked to use the restroom and that's when I got a glimpse of myself in the mirror. A nurse had to escort me to the restroom and because I was still considered a suicide risk, she had to stand inside at the door to monitor me. The first of many embarrassing moments that would occur over the next several days. Once I finished, I stood at the sink to wash my hands and I almost crumbled at the sight of myself. I looked like I had been hit by a freight train. I felt weak and dizzy. I was still drunk and in a daze from all the alcohol and pills. The nurse helped me back to my bed and then a doctor came in. He told me I was "very lucky." I wasn't trying to hear all that because deep down, I was pissed. I wanted to get my things and head on out. The doctor shared that I had a long road ahead of me and that I was not being released anytime soon. I felt the anger and frustration rising.

He stated, "Because you tried to harm yourself, we must monitor you for the next two days to make sure the pills didn't do any major harm to your vital organs. Then you'll get moved up to the psych unit. You have been Baker Acted. You'll be assessed by the psychiatrist, and we'll get you set up with the help you need. All I need from you is for you to get your rest and let us help you." The Baker Act in Florida is a law that enables families and loved ones to provide emergency mental health services and temporary detention for people who are impaired because of their mental illness, and who are unable to determine their needs for treatment.

I thought I would explode! The Baker Act? I had worked for years in the mental health arena, and I KNEW if I didn't succeed, I'd be poked, prodded, and examined for days. And held against my will. What was I thinking? I couldn't believe what was happening. I was beyond pissed at myself. Meanwhile, my aunt and uncle were encouraging me to look at this as my opportunity to get the necessary rest and resources that I needed. But mainly, you could tell that they were relieved that I was not being released and that I'd get some help.

I didn't speak much after this news. I cried for hours. Eventually, I was transferred to a secure unit where I was under medical monitoring to see how my organs would respond to the pills I had taken. I was all alone in this new private room, and I remember getting a phone call from my parents (who had literally just left the day before). I cried and cried. I kept saying that I was "sorry." My dad was so sweet as he tried to encourage me. At one point, his voice turned stern as he repeatedly told me to "stop saying you're sorry." I was deeply crushed that my sister/best friend refused to speak to me at that moment. I knew I had hurt so many people by doing this. I'm super sensitive so when I realized how much damage I had done and could have potentially done, I felt like I'd been gutted. Eventually, my sis agreed to speak with me, and I just cried. It's all I could do because I was all out of words. What got me the most was when the first psychiatrist walked into the room.

"So, Ms. Roberson, is it?" The psychiatrist didn't seem to have much of a bed-side-manner. She came in like a hurricane. I sat up in my bed.

"Yes, I'm Dana." I was nervous because I knew what was about to happen. Here comes those intrusive questions that should lead the Sherlock Holmes standing in front of me, to her big discovery about me.

"So, tell me this. What would have happened to Taz? I see here you have a teenager. Tell me what he would have done at the end of this little stunt you pulled today?"

I lost it! I hadn't thought about Taz AT ALL! It made me sick to my stomach! How could I be so selfish? I swear up until that moment, I hadn't asked about my son. I hadn't asked to reach out to my ex-husband. I typed these words through all sorts of emotions and fighting back tears recalling her questions. I would have utterly destroyed my son. The thought of how he would have had to navigate through this world without me and with the horrible looming truth that I killed myself. I would have devastated that little boy - for life! My son would have been destroyed and his life could have been marred with all of the stereotypes of mental illness - depression and sadness, as well as anger and confusion. God only knows what a loss of that magnitude would have done to him. I worked so hard to shield him from what could have eventually become his reality.

The psychiatrist and I spent a lot of time processing my guilt. We talked about what led up to my attempt to kill myself. We talked about all the things that were nagging me and causing me to want to escape. I felt awful inside, but the more we spoke, the clearer my thoughts became. Yet, during my darkest hour, that psychiatrist helped me find a glimmer of hope in my situation. Although the waves of depression still engulfed me, I saw a light. I saw a glimpse of the beauty that was going to follow this horrific episode. That was the hope that I needed to get my shit together. I learned in that first session, in that hospital bed, that every decision that I would make from that day forward would have to be deliberate and intentional. All I had to do was make the serious decision to live and make the vital decision to fight.

After my session with the hospital psychiatrist, I asked to use the phone. I needed to find out how my son was doing. I called my ex-husband who expressed a sincere concern for me. He told me that our son was doing okay and that he hadn't shared with him what was going on. He told our son that "Mommy was getting help." My heart ached so bad for my son. I thought about the weekend before and how he had seen me at my worst. I was lost in my thoughts when I heard my ex on the other end of the phone, "Dana, you just need to do what you need to do to get back on your feet. We'll tell Taz about this later, but for now just know he's fine." I felt like an idiot, but I had another pressing concern: "Can you take Taz by the house so that he can check on Maddie Merlot?" I ensured that he'd take our son by to feed our cat and clean the litter box. Priorities.

I stayed in the medical unit for three days. The first morning after I was admitted, was my 38th birthday. I lay in that hospital bed for three days straight. I was left alone with my thoughts, and boy, were they running wild. I was beating myself up for being so stupid and selfish. The guilt was debilitating. I came to the realization, while talking with the psychiatrist, that I had timed this suicide attempt exactly right, and after I had made the decision to no longer live my life hiding this secret alcohol addiction. I had flashbacks to how painful it felt when I found myself in my walk-in closet sneaking my wine in so that my son would not see that I was drinking again. I lay there in that bed with those thoughts swirling. I could get out of bed and go anywhere in the facility, but I preferred to lay there for three days barely eating, and barely sleeping because my insomnia was at an all-time high. I wasn't able to be given any medications to help me sleep until my system was cleared. It was a nightmare. What made matters worse is that, although my unit wasn't considered the psych unit, it was a lockdown area for patients being monitored and later transferred to Psych. For the life of me, I can't understand that, but let's stay on topic.

Being that there were others like me on that floor, I had an uninvited visitor every 20 minutes or so. Thank God my door was closed, but one guy kept roaming up and down the hall and he would stop in front of my door and place his face up against the small window. He just stood there and stared at me. My heart started racing because I didn't know if he was plotting and thinking about entering my room. I called the nurses' station. A nurse came and escorted the young man back to his room. He was a tall, thin Black man, with sadness and madness in his eyes. It really creeped me out and was a stark realization of what I was about to be in for when I got to the fifth floor. I had always heard that behavioral units were always on the fifth floor, and thought it was a joke, but – this unit was really on the fifth floor. The irony was overwhelming. I had only been on a Psych Ward in the professional capacity as a freaking therapist and social worker. This can't be my life!

On my third day in the medical unit, I had a few visitors come by. I won't say who these visitors were to respect their privacy, but they were the worst visitors considering my situation. I was still extremely ill and all I needed around me was love and light. The rules were that I could have visitors while I was still on the medical unit, but once I got transferred to the Psych Unit, no visitors were allowed. These visitors were important people in my life so when they showed up, I was moved, but I was also extremely uncomfortable. They were kind enough to bring me a few items like a head wrap for my hair (my hair is a whole chapter by itself); and other personal items, that I would later learn were all hazardous and had to be kept in a locker until I was discharged. Seriously? I was dealing with the worst situation in my life and all the advice, recommendations, and suggestions that came flying at me, from every angle during their visit, only made me sad. It was difficult for me to process things. My brain felt foggy and mushy at the same damn time and that's quite a disaster. I reached to turn inward and that wasn't working – there was no escape. Here's what one of my guests said to me, which caused me to kick them out:

"Life is hard. I mean, things get tough sometimes, but you don't kill yourself. You gotta be stronger than that. You see what I go through sometimes. You see the stuff I've dealt with. I would never kill myself!"

I can't put into words the emotions that were crashing up against each other and pulsating throughout my body after that unwise advice. I was so embarrassed. I felt small. I was weak, and I was angry. Before I knew it, I asked them to leave. They insisted on staying and I insisted even harder that they go. They hugged me and went on their way. I lay there in that hospital bed with my new head wrap on and cried for the remainder of the day.

I was severely depressed and had attempted suicide less than 72 hours prior. I was fragile. I did not need any lectures and I didn't need anyone telling me what they would and wouldn't do. There is a time and a place for everything. I would have received that message a lot better had I been in a different head space. I'm not going to lie, I felt extremely low, and I knew this would be the reaction from more people around me. People can be extremely judgmental, and I totally get why the topic of suicide makes people uncomfortable. It simply doesn't make sense to end your own life. No one in their right mind would do it, right? So, therein lies the irony. I began to agonize over the fact that I would forever be labeled as someone who tried to take their own life. It made my anxiety fly through the roof! To my surprise, though, I'm happy to say I was wrong about most of that. I'm also proud to say that the work that I do today is centered around breaking down the stigma around mental health issues, addictions, and suicide prevention.

That visit only added fuel to the fire and I had no idea that it would be one of the key factors in my decision to speak out and start living my life out loud.

Let the Real Treatment Begin: Welcome to the Fifth Floor

So, the day finally arrived when I would be transferred to the Psychiatric Unit. I was on an emotional rollercoaster ride. I was terrified because I always had a strange infatuation with people who end up in places like mental facilities, jails, and prisons, and I wanted to understand them. However, all I was thinking was this would be my home for the next week, and God only knew what was about to happen.

My Baker Act hadn't been lifted yet. If being on a Psych Unit was going to be anything like the movies and documentaries I had seen, I was in for it. I loved movies and documentaries on such topics, and I was always fascinated with actor Jack Nicholson's character in the psychological drama "One Who Flew Over the Cuckoo's Nest". It's a film from 1975 that explores individuality, themes, and ideas that explain human thoughts and behaviors. It looks at what makes people unique. As a result of seeing that film and, "Out of Darkness," starring actor/singer Diana Ross, I was sold on all things related to understanding the human brain and how it affects our behavior. In Ross' 1994 film, she played the role of a young woman who battled schizophrenia. I was so locked into this film because the character was a young, Black woman, and her life was very painful as she traveled the road back to sanity. The character displayed irrational, violent, and out of control behavior. It scared me because I had never seen anything like it. I have always been super inquisitive, and I love to seek knowledge on topics or anything that I do not understand. I found out that schizophrenia was a disorder in the brain, and I read all about how it affects people. I focused my undergraduate studies on psychology as my major and sociology as my minor. I wanted to be a psychiatrist because of this exposure. That would eventually change when I found out I would have to go to medical school first. I was not having that, so I went the Master of Social Work route and became a Mental Health Therapist. I ultimately landed in the pharmaceutical sales industry and was lucky to sell in the mental health world after years of proven sales success.

I mention my foundation in psychology for a specific reason. During the chaos in my life, I had been working as a representative marketing a drug for Major Depressive Disorders. My job consisted of visiting primary care offices, as well as psychiatrist's offices and promoting this medication for those patients that needed help. I developed great relationships with the doctors, nurses and staff and I helped to make sure they stayed stocked up on patient resources. I had come full circle in terms of tying my background in psychology/social work with sales. I remember an office in a rural town where they had a significant number of indigent and uninsured patients. I spent a lot of time in this office and made some great connections. My favorite nurse at this office was Rachel. She was so in control of the bedlam that took place daily. We worked very closely. I consistently checked on her needs and provided resources for the patients. Fast forward to my first day on the Psych Unit and guess who the intake nurse was - Rachel. I cannot make this stuff up.

I almost fainted when I saw her sitting on the opposite side of a desk in the intake area. She hadn't seen me yet. I was chaperoned by a medical assistant. We stood quietly as Rachel wrapped up a phone call. She grabbed a folder that was in front of her. When she finally looked up, our eyes locked. I was a hot mess. My hair was in this awful, dry afro because I had taken my weave/sew-in out a few days before my horrible, failed attempt to leave this Earth. I felt so frumpy, ugly, and disgusting. I had entered that rural office to visit with Rachel, week after week dressed to the nines, hair always laid, and on point. High heels, fresh face of make-up and a whole lot of sass. I stood there hoping she didn't recognize me in my naked rawness – no make-up or fancy clothes, and most certainly no spunky sassy attitude. I began to shrink into myself when she stood up and came from behind the desk. She didn't speak a word. Rachel walked over to me and simply embraced me in the warmest hug I had ever felt. I broke. I melted into her gentle squeeze. I let the tears flow, and I told her that I was beyond embarrassed and horrified. I didn't know what was going to be expected of me. My hands were shaking. Rachel spoke reassuringly and did not ask me any questions.

I knew that she was not judging me, and as if she was reading my mind, she said to me, "Don't feel ashamed, Dana. You're in the best place that you could be right now. Let's get this work done."

For the next several hours I went through intake. This is the initial interview where all your information is collected and confirmed. I was given a pair of light blue scrubs to change into. I had been in a hospital gown over the past few days while I was on the Medical Unit. I was eager to slip into those scrubs. I was given a pair of underwear and told that I could get more scrubs and a new pair of underwear as needed. The pair of underwear was paper thin, and I have zero idea what material was used to make those things! I was also given a small bin that contained a tiny bar of cheap soap with no fragrance, a small bottle of baby lotion, and a small toothbrush with toothpaste. This was really happening, and I was slowly starting to think this was going to be worse than I had imagined.

As if things couldn't get any worse, as I was being led to the rooms, there was a young lady having a total meltdown. The screaming and yelling threatened to send me into an inconvenient panic attack. I needed to pay attention, but that shit was distracting and horrifying. I kept my focus on the tour that Rachel was giving me. The unit was set up in a large circle. There was a huge area in the middle reserved for the nurse's workstation and private meeting rooms that the psychiatrists used. The approximately 50 rooms where patients slept were on the perimeter of that center area. The circle would become my favorite place. It was like walking around a large track. I saw patients walking laps and some of them looked zonked out, while there were others talking to themselves or looking at their imaginary friend and making hand gestures as if someone were there walking beside them. This made me feel sad. I was now among the people I had spent my whole life trying to help. I have always had a soft spot in my heart for people with mental health issues, but to be on this side of the fence felt like a cruel joke.

Once Rachel completed the tour, she guided me to my temporary home. The door to my assigned living quarters was open and I was told that the doors were to mainly stay open, however, there were times where you might need more privacy and that it was okay to close the door for a quick minute. As she spoke, I noticed there was someone else in the room and I was interested in finding out who the hell was laying on a bed in my room! My stomach dropped when I realized that I would have a freaking roommate! Things got one thousand times worse in my head. All I could think was *"awwwwww damn!"*

Rachel introduced me to the young lady named Skai who was resting in her bed curled up in a fetal position. She was facing away from the door, so when we entered the room, she had to shift her body to face Rachel and I, as we were standing near the foot of her bed. Rachel was a tiny-frame White woman whose eyes were bloodshot red. Rachel asked her if she had been "crying again" and Skai buried her face into her pillow. She let out a loud groan and my only thought was, *"here we go with this bullshit!"*

I won't lie about my feelings. I felt AWFUL. I felt ANGRY. I felt EMBARRASSED. I was anxious and felt like I needed to shed my skin. This truly felt like the worst punishment in my life. I was pissed about having a roommate because I cherish my privacy and space when I'm away from home. I always book a hotel room when I'm visiting family and friends and I'm just not one for sharing personal space. To think I'd be cramped up in a small room with this stranger for days made me want to lose my lunch. I thought to myself for the millionth time since my admission into the hospital, *"I did not think this one all the way through at all."*

Rachel checked with me to make sure that I felt comfortable with getting settled in. It's not like I had luggage or anything. It was just me, myself, and I. Oh, and all my real baggage that needed to be unpacked from this brain of mine that stemmed from years and years of living outside of my purpose. Some self-inflicted. Some heaped on me by the intruders I let into my life, but at any rate, it was time to get crackin' and I was staring my reality in the face for the first time. I had been inadvertently thrust into the role of survivor. I became a survivor of an attempted suicide, and I did not like that idea. I knew that I was going to have to muster up some amazing strength to deal with the outside world who I knew was sure to beat me up over this. I made up my mind to do whatever it was going to take to get out of this place. I was shocked at how desperate I was to escape and to what measures I'd take to get out of that Psych Unit.

Rachel left the room, and I walked over to my assigned bed which was near a window that was facing nowhere. I was already feeling my frustrations rising. I was also miserably sad. I felt down and hopeless. I realized, in that moment, that I hadn't had a single ounce of alcohol in three days. I couldn't believe it. Things had been so crazy that I didn't miss the alcohol. I also decided that I would never pick it up again. I knew that I needed to do my part while hospitalized. I was angry about that, but I knew the work had to be done. I thought about how my first stint in treatment three months ago didn't go well because once I finished the eight weeks, I didn't stay connected to any resources. I stopped going to group and individual therapy, and I did not attend AA meetings anymore because I was frustrated with trying to find the right room for me. Now, I was sitting in this Psych Unit, kicking myself for not holding on tight enough to my sobriety. I don't think it was a matter of not caring or not taking things seriously at first, but for me, it was more so about the fact that I hadn't mastered the core principles around staying sober. I hadn't settled into the idea, and I hadn't focused on strengthening my coping skills. I really thought I had control. One of the great things that would come out of this relapse and suicide attempt was the evidence that I had a long way to go. I was far from healed, and I couldn't play with my life any longer.

I spent a little time organizing the scarce personal hygiene items I'd received earlier. My sleeping area consisted of a twin-size bed with a flimsy blanket over a thin dingy white fitted sheet. I generally have a hard time sleeping so I knew that my nights in this bed were going to be a nightmare, literally. I went into the bathroom to check out the scenery. Small shower to the left, sink, then toilet. Pretty basic. I decided to keep my three-inch bar of soap, toothpaste, and toothbrush on the little nightstand next to the bed. I eventually sat down on my assigned bed and stared out the window for a while. My daydream about my freedom was interrupted by the sound of sniffles. The sniffling became increasingly closer together and louder. My roommate was bawling her eyes out by the time I walked over to try to comfort her. Skai looked up at me through tired, worn eyes. I could see she was spent from crying, and I knew that feeling all too well. I re-introduced myself to Skai. "Well, like Rachel shared, I'm Dana. Are you going to be, okay?"

Skai sat up slightly with her back up against the pillow she'd placed behind her back. I walked over to my assigned bed and sat down, facing her, and gesturing for her to start talking if she was comfortable. Skai shared her story with me, and the most puzzling feeling came over me. I was stuck on the part of Skai's story where this was her fourth suicide attempt! I was also suddenly pissed off that they thought it was okay to put a newly suicidal patient with an expert offender. The thought of this made my blood boil. I was jolted back to reality when Skai asked, "so, what you in for?"

First off, I never thought in a million-gazillion years I'd ever have that infamous question posed to me. I've watched my share of prison lock-up shows and movies about institutions, and that's question number one. I really couldn't believe this shit! I shared with Skai that I "accidentally took too many sleeping pills." The blank stare on Skai's face was quite profound and it was loud. Her facial expression screamed: "Can't bullshit a bullshitter!" I knew we were gonna be cool because she didn't even bother to challenge my lie.

Skai shared with me that she was 25 years old. My heart immediately broke when she went on to say she has a five-year-old daughter. She'd been struggling with depression her entire life, and the issues with her daughter's father were what put her over the edge. It didn't help that she also had an addiction to opioids. My heart continued to break into pieces. I couldn't imagine being suicidal at 25 years old. What was I thinking with that type of thought? I guess 38 years old was a more appropriate age to try to off yourself. My mind was still pretty jacked up. Keep in mind, I was only four days out from my incident and clearly, nothing had changed in terms of my warped thinking.

I was scheduled to meet with the psychiatrist after lunch and I was dreading it. Talking to Skai gave me a chance to deflect from my own situation, and I found myself encouraging Skai. I shared with her that my son was a teenager so I could relate to her as a mother. We shared our experiences with various medications and even started comparing efficacy and side effects. The sad reality kept sneaking up on me and all I kept thinking was, *this cannot be happening!"*

Around 11:15 a.m. a counselor showed up in our doorway. He was tall, dark, and handsome. I immediately brushed my hair back with my hand, embarrassed again that so many people were seeing me at my worst. His name was Shawn and he told Skai and I to get ready to head over to the lunchroom. There was nothing to do to prepare, except wash our hands. I offered for Skai to go into the bathroom first. I followed up and then we followed Shawn to the cafeteria/recreational room. Shawn introduced himself to me,

"I see you're new. I'm one of the counselors, Shawn. What do you like to be called?"

"Hey, I'm Dana. No nicknames." I was not excited about the possibility of him prying into my life.

Shawn ushered Skai and I into the corridor outside of the cafeteria where we joined other patients in line. Shawn told me to grab my tray and go into the cafeteria when it was my turn. I was so afraid of what this experience was about to be. I noticed Skai had made her way to the front of the line where she was met by someone she knew. Skai was leaning on this young woman's shoulder and the woman was stroking Skai's hair. I was nervous about where I would sit and knowing who in the hell was sane or not? I knew I was sane, but would others assume that I'm not? Just like I was assuming they were all basket cases. What a disaster!

My turn came to grab a tray from a food serving rack. There were no options. Basically, you get what's served. I barely looked down at my tray because I was horrified at the idea of having so sit with strangers and eat my food. To my surprise, as soon as I walked in, Skai stood halfway from her seat and signaled for me to come over and sit with her and four others. There was a young lady with purple hair, tons of tattoos and piercings everywhere. I learned that she called herself "Rainbow Bright."

I met Nicolas who sat to the right of Skai. He looked young and had beautiful piercing blue eyes with long blonde hair. He was a young professional who had battled drug addiction since he graduated from college and entered the workforce. Eazey was the 40-year-old White dude with black-rimmed glasses. He was very handsome; his eyeglasses made him look studious. But what I'd come to learn about Eazey is that he had zero desire to live. His wife and his newborn son were the only reason he was still breathing but he still battled the intrusive thoughts of suicidal ideation and he continuously found himself voluntarily checking himself into treatment for help. Finally, there was Tristan. Tristan was a college student who had been struggling with mental health issues since he was eight years old. He was 23 years old and trying to complete his graduate degree. I had been thrust into an environment surrounded by case studies and my mind was doing somersaults. Again, my brain was in rescue mode, but that would quickly change after those psychiatrists got a hold of me.

Lunch was uneventful during the first 15 minutes or so. Then, as if they were cued, two patients across the room started pulling and tugging at each other's hair. These two women were screaming profanities at one another and fighting off anyone who tried to break them apart. It was quite amusing at first, but then things started to escalate. Then the ripple effect started. All I know is that I felt a rush of air fly past me as four young men came flying by our table. They all leaped and jumped into the middle of the pile of humans where the fight broke out. I grabbed my tray and made my way to the exit. One of the counselors stopped me and others at the door. The counselor was Mr. Simms, a young college student who worked there to pay for his education. Mr. Simms' face was as red as a tomato as he yelled for us to return to our seats. By now, several counselors were ushering the fight club out of the cafeteria. My heart was racing, and I feared for my life. What the hell was going on?

Once things calmed down, we were instructed to eat our food and not speak to one another. We were on lockdown which meant once we ate our lunch, we were escorted back to our rooms and told to stay until the lockdown was lifted. Thankfully, for me, this meant it was time for my appointment with the psychiatrist.

I had to wait for one of the counselors to escort me, but they were tied up after the fight. I was a little anxious about being late for my appointment, but I actually arrived on time. The psychiatrist sat in a corner cubicle, and he had a chair pulled up beside him. He looked up and signaled for me to join him. There were five other cubicles lining the perimeter of the room. There were two other psychiatrists talking with patients. I made my way over to the man and he stood to greet me and through a warm smile, stated, "Hey, I'm Dr. Raven. I'm here to help get you back on track and back to living your life. How does that sound?"

My heart smiled a little, but it didn't transfer to my face. I felt flat and had no emotion to offer this doctor. Then it hit me – If my memory serves me right, this doctor has complete control over whether-or-not I can get out of this place. I immediately changed my tune, "Hi, I'm Dana. I made a mistake and took too many sleeping pills. I was exhausted and I didn't realize I had taken so many. I just needed sleep."

The doctor allowed his blank stare to linger a little too long for my comfort level. His blank stare was one that forced me to start digging myself out of this ridiculous hole I had dug for myself. The doctor let the silence permeate through the air. The air was getting thick, but I wasn't budging, and neither was he. Then, for dramatics, I suppose, as soon as I opened my mouth and began to explain myself again, the doctor cut me off, "Dana, I have a copy of your suicide note."

That was my sign to start explaining the purpose behind my suicide attempt. I dug deep and tried with all my heart to sort through my thoughts and feelings. It's hard to put into words how this felt for me, but I'll try. You wake up from a chaotic, crazy dream where everything around you is moving too fast, but you know you must reach out and grip something…. anything… to keep from being sucked up into the chaos. So, you grab onto something that feels soothing, comforting, safe. It feels secure. But then you start to lose your grip. Things are moving too fast again! Now, you're frantically searching for the next best thing to grab a hold of. Where is that sturdy, strong, support? This goes on repeatedly until you feel like the only option is to give up. Or like it's not worth it anymore. So, you decide to let go. You decide to end a chaotic cycle.

Although he provided a safe place for me to start slowly, I was not able to verbalize this during my first session with the doctor. During the first session, I shared the details and dynamics of my family. I shared details about my childhood and what type of values and morals I live by. Being that I had studied to become a therapist, I was familiar with this model of treatment, and it kept hitting me from every angle that I was now the client and I needed to trust these practitioners. They always say teachers are the worst students and health care professionals are the worst patients. Therapists make the worst clients, too.

Eventually, my session ended, and Dr. Raven gave me an assignment to complete before our next appointment the following afternoon. I asked him if there was any way to get a pen and paper. I felt a strong urge to write. Dr. Raven said he'd have one of the counselors bring them to me. I was escorted back to my room by a counselor named Addison, who remained quiet as she walked slightly ahead of me. It was a little after 2 p.m. and I was curious about what the rest of my day would entail. I asked Addison what was next, and she said Group Therapy and Activity Hour were starting at 3 p.m. so I had time to either hang out in my room or in the common gathering area where the television is. There were no televisions in the personal rooms and if you chose to go into the common area, you were stuck watching whatever was on until eventually you would get to witness a daily World Wrestling Entertainment match between the residents.

I waited in my room, lying on my left side staring out the window at the brick wall next door. The irony. Literally staring into nothingness. That brick wall symbolized something for me. This is what I thought to myself: *"Okay, you've hit a brick wall. You didn't shatter into a million little pieces. You're still here. You have an opportunity to pull yourself up and get it right this time. The way you move forward depends solely on how you respond to this treatment that you are being offered. This is your lifeline. Use it and move forward. There is nothing left in your past to try to rectify or make sense of. You have the chance to make this life more meaningful than it's ever been before. You have an assignment that you must fulfill. Let's get crackin'!"*

Right before the group began, Shawn, the counselor, tapped on the door which was slightly ajar. Skai and I both turned toward the door. Shawn's hand was outstretched and there was a small black and white composition notebook and a small half-sized pencil with no eraser. It was one of those tiny pencils you give toddlers when they are learning how to write. I got up from my bed and made my way over to retrieve my gifts from Shawn. I thanked him and placed them onto the nightstand. Shawn told Skai and I to go ahead and get ready to head to group, and that he would escort us since he was already there. I went into the bathroom to wash my hands and slick my afro back with some water and the baby lotion I'd been given. I still looked like a hot mess, but I must admit, I really didn't give a damn.

On the way to group therapy, Shawn asked, "so what do you plan to do with the notebook and pencil? You an artist?"

I responded with no excitement, "Just need to get my thoughts out. I've always kept a journal. I sorta think this might be the ideal time to take advantage of that."

Shawn detected the hint of sarcasm and we both giggled. Skai was dragging 12 steps behind us. God only knows what she was back there thinking. I noticed my behavior immediately. Here I was trying to align myself with the staff because technically I was more qualified, educated, and trained than half of them. Then when it came to the few interactions that I had already had with some of the patients, I was slowly diagnosing and formulating a treatment plan in my head for each of them. Meanwhile, back at the ranch, I was the main one in need of refuge and rescue. I would eventually be jolted back to reality.

My first group therapy session was painful. I was in complete denial of my situation. I sat quietly at one of the tables that lined the cafeteria. It was the same place where we'd had our lunch. I did not participate in the group discussions. After 30 minutes of bantering and ideas and stories being thrown around, we were given 30 minutes of recreation time. I got up from the table and roamed around the room. There were board games, puzzles, cards, construction paper, markers and crayons strewn throughout the room on top of the tables. I found my way to a Scrabble game at the end of one of the tables. I thought playing a word scrambling game by myself would be great. Not even ten seconds after I'd gotten the letter tiles out of the box, a young man plopped down at the table right across from me. He started grabbing some of the letters. I knew I would have to play it cool because he was one of the residents I had seen before having a melt down and needing intervention. I decided to play nicely.

I asked him what his name was, "They call me Poppa, what's your name?" Poppa was picking at a scab on his elbow. He looked multiracial and had exceptionally light skin. His hair was silky and curly, and the ringlets hung loosely all over his head. He had big deep-set eyes that told a story. There seemed to be a sadness lurking, however, he excitedly awaited my response.

I responded, "I'm Dana. I must warn you; I really don't know how to play Scrabble. I was just going to play around and see how many words I can spell."

To my surprise, this elated Poppa! We burst out into laughter as he shouted out, "Fuck the rules! We doin' it our way today!" With that, Poppa spelled out his first word from the tiles in front of him, "D-O-G" and slammed his fist on the table, shaking the tiles. He yelled out in amusement as loud as he could, "BINGO!!!!" I knew at that moment the party was just getting started and I wanted nothing more than to find the nearest exit.

I allowed Poppa to entertain me as we both spelled out all sorts of words. I liked that I was distracted for an entire 30 minutes and was not focused on my reality. As soon as recreation time was over, my mood immediately shifted back to sad and desolate. I was getting nervous about how my first night on this unit would go. I mentioned to the psychiatrist earlier how I hadn't slept in years. She prescribed a sleeping agent for me so I was preoccupied with whether it would work. I needed something to knock me out. It was in moments like this that I would think about how alcohol did the trick for me in terms of escaping. I still couldn't believe I hadn't had a lick of alcohol in days. I was also worried about dinner. I hadn't eaten much at lunch due to all the crazy outbursts and I hadn't had much of an appetite since I'd been admitted days ago. After group we had one hour before dinner would be served. We were escorted back to our rooms, and given the option to hang out in them, walk the circle, or lounge in the TV area. I decided to take a few laps around the circle.

I started out on my own. I felt so uncomfortable. I was the new girl, and everyone had been checking me out all day. I quickly found out it was everyone's goal to find out what the new person was in for. So random patients would come alongside me and try to join me on my stroll. At first, I had a hard time swatting them away. Take Alicia for example:

Alicia was a hefty young Black girl. She barged in on my little walk from out of nowhere. She fell in lock step with me and started blabbing. I could tell she was young, but I also noticed some mental health issues right away. She went on and on about how she likes to fight so she can be my protector. As soon as she revealed this fun trait, it hit me that she was the one throwing a conniption when I arrived at the unit earlier that day. I braced myself because I knew she wouldn't go away easily. I went into therapist mode and started asking open-ended questions; trying to lead her away by asking her what she normally does between group therapy and dinner time. That method didn't work worth a damn. It gave her more energy and excitement. We were quickly becoming besties and I knew I had to act. I eventually told her that I had some deep thinking that I needed to do before it was time for dinner, and it was important that I do it alone. Alicia gave me an odd stare as she twisted the braids in her hair. She suddenly came to a screeching halt. I stopped and turned to look at her and she simply walked away. *"Well, I'll be damned,"* is all I could think.

Not even 15 minutes after I had given Alicia her walking papers, a tall, fit nice-looking White dude stepped out of his doorway and got into unison with me. It was obvious he had seen me pass by a few times with Alicia. He had timed it exactly right and as he joined me; he stuck his hand out for me to shake, "Hey, I'm Alex."

Alex wore dark-rimmed glasses like Clark Kent in the comic book series "Superman". I don't know why I felt a connection, but I eagerly shook Alex's hand and told him he was welcomed to join me. Something felt normal about him, and I was hoping he could shield me from the others that were trying to get access to me.

Alex didn't disappoint. We quickly became buddies during that initial walk together. We chatted about what landed us in this place that most, unfortunately, called the "nut house". As it turned out, Alex was severely depressed, and no medication or treatments had helped him thus far. He was 35 years old and was holding on by a thread with his marriage, his kids, and his job. Alex was an Emergency Medical Technician, and I could tell he really loved his job. His biggest problem was substance abuse because it was the only thing that helped him feel better about life. His drug of choice was heroin. My heart ached as I listened to Alex share his story. One thing I knew was that he was beyond resilient. When you meet people in a place like this, you know that there is a God, and He plucks us out of the thickness of our addictions and gives us a new life. I began praying for that outcome for Alex.

I found myself doing what I always do when I meet someone new. I was asking a million questions. I work hard not to do that because previously I would find myself in sticky situations. I thank God that I have this natural affinity to help others, but sometimes it can feel like another addiction for me. I wish I didn't care about other people so much. One might call it being nosey, others may call it a genuine love for learning about the lives and experiences of others. And then there's me who will get someone to bare their soul in under one hour. Then I take on their worries and make them my own. I brainstorm at a million miles a minute to try to help produce a solution and I want to make sure that person no longer feels stressed, sad, or mad. I beg God to take this away from me because it's exhausting at times. I just don't know when to say, "that really doesn't concern me." Alex was talking 90 miles per minute and seemed to be enjoying our little impromptu counseling session.

Eventually it was time to prepare for dinner, so Alex and I agreed to meet up in the cafeteria and sit together. I noticed a spark in his voice and a change in his demeanor. Could we both be feeling like there's a light at the end of the tunnel on this depression train? I had no idea how much Alex and I would come to rely on each other over the next several days. Sometimes you can feel when you've found your people. Alex was my people.

I went to my room to wash my hands and wait to be escorted to dinner. I was feeling anxious again. Dinnertime was another one of the firsts in my first day on the unit. I calmed down a bit, remembering that Alex and I had a date. I had to find a little excitement in something in that place. If it meant psyching myself up, then that's what I did. That way of coping became a large part of how I continue to heal. I was able to learn how to monitor my thinking, which in turn directly affects my mood and my attitude.

Once I got to dinner, I moved through the line eager to see what we were having. The hospital food hadn't been horrible on the Medical Unit, and I was hoping we'd be eating the same types of meals. It was just as I expected. Nothing like what I had been able to experience while on the Medical Unit. At least when I was there, I was able to select what I wanted. I had at least two or three options. Not here. I don't even want to get into the rationale behind that, but I did force myself to imagine what it would be like allowing 41 psych patients to decide what they wanted for lunch and dinner with limited options. Take the options away, and voila, you've got compliance.

That particular night was Salisbury steak, mashed potatoes, and green beans. I wanted to crawl into a hole. I met up with Alex and immediately drilled him about the food being served. Alex was reassuring and told me we will have snack time and positive affirmations before lights out, which is at 9 p.m. He told me to get excited about graham crackers and peanut butter. I had never had that combination before, but the way my stomach was growling and my mind was winning the battle to not eat the garbage in front of me, I started to get really excited about those graham crackers and peanut butter.

Later that night, after I had taken my first shower and gotten myself in line for medication, I felt an awful gnawing feeling in the pit of my gut. I was ACTUALLY in the Psychiatric Unit! I was in line chatting with Alex, watching as one lifeless and numb patient after the next stepped up to the medication window. I watched as each person was handed a tiny white paper cup. It was fascinating to see how each patient would look down into their cup as if to ask, "do I really need this?" The ones who caused too much fuss were escorted away. I watched as they rationalized in their head that this battle couldn't be won, they swallowed the pills down with the small cup of water provided, and then, the infamous lifting up of the tongue, wiggling it around, and yelling, "aaaaaaaahhhhhhhh." I couldn't believe this shit. But this was my reality, so, I stepped right up when it was my turn. I was told I was being given medication to help me sleep in addition to a new medication that would help with my depression. "Do you have any questions?" the nurse asked. In my head, I heard my voice yelling, *"Nope! I hope this shit knocks me the fuck out!"*

I was nervous about what was going to happen that night. I took the medication hoping and praying that it would help me forget about everything in my life at that moment. My anxiety was extremely high, so I trusted in that medication – I was desperate. I had to lift and wiggle my tongue just like everyone else and it felt somewhat degrading. I think what I was going through was the frightening realization that I was no different than anyone in that unit. We all had a mental health issue and/or addictions of some sort and we all needed help. That's what I learned in that moment standing in line to get my medication. Perfectionism was completely out the window.

We had one hour before the lights went out and we were all ushered to the cafeteria/activity room. We were told to have a seat at a table and each table was invited up to the front one at a time to retrieve snacks. When Alex said we were going to have graham crackers and peanut butter I thought that was going to be the only option. To my surprise, there were other options including applesauce, peanut butter crackers, and juice. I saw others smearing the peanut butter on their graham crackers and they looked like they were enjoying it. I decided to try it, and I must admit that became my new favorite snack. For the next four days that would be the highlight of my day – getting my snack and taking my ass to bed. And guess what I threw in my buggy at the grocery store the first chance I got upon my release? Graham crackers and peanut butter!

C H A P T E R   9

Precious Sleep! Laaaaaawd, I Thank Ya!

That first night I must admit I was horrified. My roommate and I did not speak much because she was having another meltdown and all I could do was encourage her to try to get some sleep and know that tomorrow is another day. I remember laying there for about 30 minutes or so before the lights went out and I grabbed my tablet and my pencil, and I began to write. In that moment I felt completely lost. The symptoms of alcohol withdrawal were in full effect, and I was feeling extremely depressed. The medication that I was given to help me sleep kicked in quickly, especially after the graham crackers and peanut butter. After I wrote two pages in my new journal, I decided to give in to sleep. I woke up the next morning amazed that I had slept through the entire night! I did not get up to use the restroom one single time, nor did I toss and turn, or wake up prematurely. I can't tell you how amazing that felt. I couldn't believe that my body took the time to rest properly, and if nothing else, that gave me the motivation that I needed to face everything that was going on around me. I knew then that there was hope. Sleeping through the night was proof that something could aid me in tackling the issues that I had been dealing with and for me that meant it was possible to get back on track and take my life back. I think it's safe to say I was getting my optimism back. Most people who know me know that I'm typically incredibly positive and optimistic. But what depression had done was almost snuffed out my light. So even amid my darkness I know that God was leading me and guiding me back to that light. That's the light that shines in me today.

My second day on the unit was uneventful. I got up early, took my shower, and put on my blue scrubs for the day. (Real quick about those showers. Those little bars of soap that they gave us were awful. They smelled like hospital soap, and they only lasted for one shower). I remember the night before feeling so frustrated because I'm so used to having my own products, and there are certain items that I use to care for myself. This was a wakeup call that I could never find myself here again. The small container of baby lotion that I was given was already almost gone. I was only able to use it twice. That's because I use lotion every day on every inch of my body, and I was forced to use it in my hair. My hair is so thick, and it felt so dry because I hadn't moisturized it all week. Since I'd been in the hospital I came up with an idea. I asked one of the counselors to bring me extra lotion so that I could do my hair. To my surprise she gave me four bottles of little lotion and guess what, I twisted my hair into little twists by mixing the lotion with a little bit of water. That is what we call "Black Girl Magic". That made an immediate difference in how I felt going out into the unit on that second day. I can't say that I felt like myself, however, I felt more presentable. It was not necessarily about aesthetics for me, it was more about routine and having been raised to "always look presentable, no matter what." So, even then, it was important for me to look put together, when I had completely fallen apart. To walk around with my hair sticking up on my head like a chicken was not the business. So, thanks to baby lotion, I felt somewhat normal again. Yet, that was a true sign that perfectionism was still heavily lingering and very much alive.

For the next three days I would do the same routine. I would wake up from a wonderful sleep, take a shower with the itty-bitty soap, moisturize my hair with baby lotion and water, put on my blue scrubs and plastic underwear, and get to work. By then I had mastered the schedule of going to breakfast, nibbling on some eggs and fruit, and checking the boxes in terms of my treatment for the day. The reason I phrase it this way is because in no way, at no point, was I ever excited about being locked in this unit. I was simply trying to figure out how to get out sooner than my release date. When you are Baker Acted, you are held in the Psych Unit for at least 72-hours. Since I had come from the Medical Unit, my time didn't start until the day I was transferred to Psych. I had already started the countdown. I also recognize as I look back, I was plotting and had no problem with the idea of lying and being manipulative. I knew this was not an option if I genuinely wanted to heal properly.

My work with Dr. Raven improved each day. By day two I was extremely comfortable exploring the root cause of my depression. We also spent an extensive amount of time discussing the fact that I had a problem with alcohol. Dr. Raven helped me recognize why I was using alcohol to cope with the stressors in my life. At one point he asked me to describe the physical reaction of my body when I start to drink alcohol. He made me start from the very beginning. Not the lifting of the glass to my lips. I'm talking about the first thought that hits me when I know it's time for a drink. We walked through the process of going to purchase alcohol, the thrill of driving home to drink the alcohol, the feeling I got when I put the ice cubes in the glass. What does that sound like? What are you feeling? You pour the alcohol into the glass, you smell the aroma, you begin to stir, and then you bring the glass to your lips. What are you thinking, what are you feeling, what is your goal? It was these questions and analysis that helped me realize what happens when someone develops an addiction. I had never stopped to think about the whole series of events and how it was a part of the addiction. From the first thought of drinking alcohol all the way to the last sip. This exercise was amazing and there was a lot of homework I was given. This would be work that I would do over the next several months in addition to starting treatment outside of the hospital.

While on the unit I was not able to make phone calls or talk to anyone outside. The agony of not knowing how my son was doing was giving me more motivation to work hard and proved that I was ready to get back to my life. I missed my mom, my dad, and my siblings. I learned that my psychiatrist spoke with my sister and my ex-husband in the beginning of my treatment because their information was listed in my chart as my emergency contacts. My sister had agreed that I needed to stay in the hospital until my treatment was complete. At the time, I was sad about that but then when I look back, I'm extremely thankful that she was bold enough to recognize I needed help and to accept it. I wrote about that in my journal because it helped me to process my feelings and prepare myself for what was awaiting. I knew that I was going to have to go back to a reality that hadn't changed but my ability to cope with it was what was most important, and I would surely be put to the test.

My focus became all about how I wanted to move forward in my life. The psychiatrist helped me to navigate through the various scenarios that I would most certainly find myself in some days. Things related to the stress of having a job, being a single mother, and fighting to maintain my mental health. I felt confident about being released because I had already been set up to restart my treatment at Breakthroughs. I had mixed feelings about this because initially I was embarrassed. I graduated from the treatment program less than a month prior to the new incident. But I'm thankful that things turned out for me in terms of my entire treatment experience. As much as I was embarrassed to face the counselors there, I knew they had seen returning clients a million times before and it was nothing new. It still made me uncomfortable to know that I would have to sit in those rooms again and go through the process all over again. My psychiatrist encouraged me to think positively, and to know that the tools I was being given could help assure I live a much better life.

Alex and I had developed a great connection over the days that I was on the Psychiatric Unit. We encouraged each other to push through this thing called life. I was sad to have to leave Alex because he was not getting out anytime soon. He had a long road ahead of him and it made me sad for him but hopeful at the same time. He loved his kids, and he loved his wife, and you could tell he wanted to live. He was fighting hard to survive from the weight of depression. I didn't talk to many other people while I was there because I wanted to avoid any foolishness, although I did manage to develop relationships with a few of the counselors. I found myself giving advice to several of them. For instance, there were two young counselors who were working as interns while working on their bachelor's degrees. They had lots of questions for me about earning their master's degree once they learned that I had my Master of Social Work. There was a bit of irony to this but because I believe in God, I've always said that I'm right where I need to be. So even in that moment as the patient I was living in my purpose.

Release day finally came. I received the stamp of approval indicating that I had gotten my marbles back. I was beyond thrilled but frightened at the same time. My uncle agreed to pick me up, and I remember feeling so depressed. I can't explain enough how much the embarrassment was weighing on me and I knew that the conversation was going to begin upon leaving that hospital. The numerous conversations about how I "shouldn't do this" and I "shouldn't try to hurt myself" and "do you realize who you could have hurt?" What I also didn't know at the time is that just because I had been in treatment for seven days, did not mean I was miraculously cured. No one waved this mental-health-magic-wand over my brain and said, "Voila! You're healed!" There was still so much work to do and there were still so many symptoms that I had to manage, one of the most critical being my depressive symptoms. The darkness was thick. I was still dealing with the physical symptoms of depression. The medication was on board, but it typically takes up to two weeks for anti-depressants to start working in patients. The good thing was I had been sleeping well, and I could slowly feel my energy level rising. Depression zaps your energy and for a long time I was running on empty and didn't realize it. I take that back. I really thought I could do it all. I've often heard that your body will speak to you, and my whole body was shutting down on me starting with my brain. My stint in the hospital at that time was exactly what I needed to get me started on the right track. It isn't the most ideal situation, and I never would have planned it for myself but, when I look back on those seven days in the hospital, after that horrible day that I decided to end my life, I knew that my life was just beginning.

C H A P T E R   1 0

Back To Reality: The Alcohol and Streets Are Calling

I will forever remember this part of my journey. When my uncle came to pick me up from the hospital, he had to meet with a nurse and the psychiatrist first. Apparently, they gave him specific instructions on how to monitor me. I live alone; therefore, it was critical that I had someone checking in on me frequently. I really didn't want anyone worrying about me, but I had to agree to a plan in order to be released. My sick brain was still in charge and whispering that I was going to become a burden. I also must admit that I still didn't trust myself, but deep down, I knew I had to fight for my son.

My uncle was so gentle with me. He made sure I had all my belongings. I felt uncomfortable because I was wearing the same sundress that I had been brought in wearing and I had not been wearing a bra, panties, or shoes. Apparently, my sundress had been laundered, so at least it was clean. So, hospital plastic underwear and fall-risk-socks for the win! Yeah, and then on top of that the little Medusa braids I had thrown in my head made the look complete. Thankfully, I located the head scarf given to me by one of my earlier guests, which was taken from me when I entered the unit. My uncle led me to his truck that was out front in the patient pick-up area. I know my uncle very well, so I could tell his heart

101

was aching for me. I could see the hurt in his eyes. My thoughts were so scattered because it felt like a battle in my mind. One part of me was afraid to speak. How do I explain what happened? This is the uncle that I talked to about almost everything when we'd meet up once a month to catch up on life and motivate one another to keep pushing in Corporate America. He was a part of my close-knit circle. He literally saved me on so many occasions, and he didn't even know it. I'm sure he was riddled with curiosity and confusion. Then the other part of me was ready to defend myself. I had no idea how this car ride home would go, but either way, I had prepared myself.

To my surprise, my uncle played gospel music softly in the background as he shared with me that he had taken the morning off so he could help me get settled at home. I protested. I wanted to be alone. I wanted to climb into my own bed and simply rest. That was depression still heavily in play. I didn't win that battle. My uncle spoke to me about how he admired my strength. I was confused at first. He went on to say that what I had gone through made him think about his own life. It made him realize how important it is for us to reach out for help and talk to others. That was surprising yet reassuring. In my darkest hour, my uncle was pouring into me. He shared that he could relate to the fears that I had leading up to my suicide attempt and that helped us to connect. I thought about all the times we met up for hours and laughed and talked – sometimes even cried. I never told my uncle that I was struggling the way I was. He has always been a listening ear, but for some reason, I hadn't chosen to reach out to anyone for help in the past. But moving forward, reaching out for help would be my lifeline.

Once we arrived at my home my uncle helped me get inside. What I saw upon entering my house was dismaying. The furniture had been moved around so that the ambulance could get the gurney into my front door, through the living room, and onto my patio where I apparently lay passed out on my favorite chair. It was like trying to relive the most critical moment in your life yet not being able to piece it all together. I don't recall the ambulance being at my home at all. I don't remember anything up until I woke up in the hospital. So, to see barstools in the living room and the couches rearranged, made my heart ache. I put my things down and immediately started putting things back in place. I found Maddie Merlot, and she was so affectionate toward me. I even almost left this little fur baby and that wasn't fair. My brain was starting to kick into high gear with the thoughts of guilt. Rule number one that I had learned in therapy: Address the feeling head on. I asked myself why was I feeling guilty? I reminded myself that I was "sick." And I busied myself with getting my house back organized.

My uncle jumped right in and started helping me. He went into my office and started moving boxes out into my garage and sorting my work things that were in disarray. At one point I went out into the garage to check on my uncle and I saw him hard at work breaking down boxes and physically clearing any clutter. For a minute he didn't notice I was there, and I stood there thankful, receiving his help. This is what it feels like to allow help and be okay with receiving it.

After a while we were done cleaning, and my uncle was headed out. He told me he would check on me in a few hours. I told him I was going to rest and then get ready to figure out when I could get my son. I was worried that my ex-husband would want to keep my son away from me for now, but to my surprise he knew that it was important for my son and I to see one another. My ex-husband and I discussed how we would explain things to our son who had lots of questions. We felt it was important for him to understand that I was receiving help and that he did not have to worry, but I followed the recommendation of the psychiatrist that I allow my therapist to guide me in that discussion with my son. It was a scary topic for a child, and we needed to make sure the message was clear that my son was safe with me, and I would be back to my old self again soon. Again, the guilt would creep in when I thought of how things might go with my son later. I asked myself, *"why are you still beating yourself up over this?"* I knew that I would get to hug my son and kiss his sweet little face that afternoon. That warmed my heart, and I knew that's the place where I needed to start.

I can't say that I got much sleep that first day back at home. I was eagerly trying to track down my cell phone and thankfully, I still had a land line at the time. I was able to call my ex-husband and find out that his sister had my cell phone. He also confirmed with me that he felt safe with me getting our son later in the day. I was more than excited. I was able to track my phone to my niece who met up with me at a grocery store parking lot early afternoon. When my niece pulled up beside my parked car, I could see the pity in her eyes. She got out of her car and walked over toward mine. I got out of the car because her arms were outstretched into a pre-hug. It felt nice to be embraced – my second hug of the day. My niece didn't ask any questions and I was relieved. She basically embraced me, handed me my phone, and told me that her mom (my ex's sister) said to call her if I needed anything at all. I expressed my gratitude, we hugged again, and then we went our way.

My next stop was to go home and get my phone charged up. It was completely dead and unfortunately, I was locked out because amid the initial emergency, my ex-husband and his family had tried to get into my phone for emergency contacts. Do you want to hear something eerie? In that moment, I had a flashback to one of the last final actions I took before I texted my ex to let him know I was saying goodbye. I remember going through my cell phone and wiping it clean. All text messages, call histories, pictures, videos. My heart began to race at the realization that I had been sick, and I was extremely serious about ending things. I was on a mission to leave this Earth without a trace. I quickly snapped back to what was in front of me. That's a coping mechanism I had worked on often with the psychiatrist.

I had to work extra hard to control the intrusive thoughts. When those negative thoughts come, you have a choice. You can choose to sit with them and go on a magical carpet ride that always leads to anxiety (and depression in my case); or you can dismiss it right away and replace it with a more positive thought or activity.

I was able to get my cell phone open after using my landline to call the phone company. It was so important that I started making phone calls. In retrospect, I wish I had waited to make those calls. Instead, I had swung into one of my manic episodes and spent the entire afternoon calling all my family members, friends, and even coworkers, informing them of where I had been for the past week and what I had experienced. Several of my friends had reached out to me at various times, and the text and voice messages were many. People checking in and trying to find out where I was. No answers, no posts on social media. People were reaching out to one another asking if they'd heard from me. So, I owed them an explanation. Here's how I've been able to rationalize this:

I was putting guard rails in place. I wanted everyone around me to know my ugly secret right away. There was no need to be secretive and hide. I was emboldened to speak up for something. I didn't know what yet. But the reality is, I wanted people to know so that they could stay connected to me. I knew that if I had enough people praying for me and pulling for me, I'd survive. I look back on that afternoon, and it brings tears to my eyes. I had the same conversation repeatedly, uttering those nasty words, "kill myself; hurt myself; pills; alcohol; suicide."

Each reaction was unique. There were a lot of tears. A lot of my friends, literally, yelled out in shock and started to sob. I kept consoling everyone and sharing with them that I had already started my healing journey. I also got a lot of tongue lashings that day, "Dana, why didn't you call me?" "Listen, if you ever feel like that again, you call me, okay?" "What were you thinking?"

A lot of the people I phoned during that manic episode are no longer a part of my life. I didn't have to yell my business from the mountaintop that day, but I'm glad I did. People's true colors were revealed. The relationships that ended over the years were not related to my alcoholism and attempted suicide; it was more gradual since a lot of us simply grew apart. My life had to change in a drastic way which meant certain people, places, and things had to be eliminated. I was not ready for that, but it was a vital part of my healing. Everybody can't go where you need to go.

I felt relieved every time I shared my story with one of my family members or friends that day. I eventually reached the end of the list of people that I thought I should inform. After some time on that task, it was time to get prepared to pick my son up from school. I was super excited about seeing him, but I also felt a sense of shame and embarrassment. The anxiety was palpable. Surprisingly, the evening with my son was amazing and it was exactly what I needed. I fought back tears hugging him tightly that evening and assuring him things would be better. I asked if he was up for pizza and a movie. We picked up our favorite Chicago pizza, went home, and I let him pick the movie. That night, we didn't discuss the details of where I had been. My son had more questions about what was going to happen next. He never focused on what happened or where I had been. He was more concerned with our present moment and where we were headed. I also think he was fearful of the person he had seen prior to my hospitalization. That person who was drunk off her ass and didn't care about anyone or anything else. The thought of my behavior and how it affected him was agonizing. Again, I had to regain my focus and utilize the coping skills I had learned. I needed to shift my thoughts and flood my mind with positive thoughts. Here I was spending time with my son versus where I had been the night before. I was free and I had the power and the opportunity to straighten my life out. I made up my mind that night to be as optimistic as I could be.

Once the night slowed down and it was time for my son to go to bed, I felt a rush of emotions. I started to crave alcohol. Thankfully, I was prepared for this. The counselors and psychiatrist helped me to practice better coping skills. I had several options that first night back at home and I put them to use. I started writing in my journal which allowed me to sift through my thoughts and feelings. More than anything, I felt overwhelmed. I felt shame and guilt about returning to Breakthroughs the next morning to restart the treatment program. I had no idea how I would be received, and I wondered if people there had lost hope in me. Little did I know, relapses happen every day. I was no different from others seeking help for their addictions. I had no alcohol in my house at the time and I refused the urge to hop in my car and drive the one mile to Publix and purchase any. Instead, I went onto my patio and smoked a cigarette. I noticed immediately how calm I felt. I hated cigarettes with a passion, yet it was the one vice that felt safe at the time. I still needed something to numb me and take the pain away, and cigarettes would have to do.

I was given two prescriptions, as well as samples of the sleep medication and anti-depressants upon leaving the hospital. Earlier that day, I had dropped my scripts off and planned to pick up the medication the next day from my pharmacy. I took the medication for sleep and the anti-depressant that night. It was the first time I had slept in my bed in months (I often fell asleep on my couch during my heavy drinking days). So sleeping in my bed restfully felt totally awesome! The next morning, I woke up feeling refreshed and rested. I woke up early and got breakfast ready for my son. I showered and made sure I was presentable for my group therapy session that was from 9 a.m. until 12 p.m. I was less than excited, but I had already said my prayers to God. I simply asked for the courage I needed to start the treatment process again.

My son and I held hands and prayed before we left our house that morning. My son's prayer was beyond perfect. He always asked God to protect his mom and dad, but that morning, God received a more special and detailed request. My son asked for God to help "Mommy stay happy." I knew his young mind couldn't comprehend what was going on around him and he found safety and comfort in God. This was my second realization of how horrible this may have impacted my son. The first was while in the hospital when the psychiatrist entered my room for the first time and led with, "so, what would have happened to Taz?" The guilt was riveting.

After we prayed, we drove to his school with our favorite gospel songs playing in the background. We had a lively discussion about the upcoming weekend and how we were going to go to the beach. I was trying so hard to make sure my son was doing well with the situation. I couldn't imagine what he was truly feeling. I would find out several years later what exactly was going through my son's mind because as he grew and became an adult, it's something we discussed on occasion; and we continue to discuss to this day. Mental health and addictions awareness quickly became my passion and I'm so thankful for the testimony God placed in me. My son helped me to fight and I'm beyond thankful for him.

Once I dropped my son off at school, I headed to Breakthroughs. I was extremely nervous because I didn't want to deal with the humiliation of having to return. I had an hour and a half before group therapy would start, so I went to a coffee shop nearby. I went inside and ordered coffee and found a table in the corner. I pulled out my cell phone and went onto my social media pages. I hadn't been on any of my social media platforms since prior to my hospitalization. I was typically active on my different pages, sharing fun and motivational quotes, so I was not surprised when I saw that I had several messages waiting for me. They were mainly from friends of mine who were wondering where I had been for the past week. I didn't reply to anyone right away. I shifted my focus back to preparing my mind for group therapy. I was praying that there would be a new group of members, but the chances of that being the case were slim. There were several members who had been there for several months when I attended the first time. My mind flashed to an image of me sitting in that circle forever. The thought of it horrified me. I chose then to fight with all my might. I was going to be sober and alcohol free from this day forward. That was my promise to myself as I entered treatment for the second time.

For me to change the trajectory of my life, I needed to get serious. There was no room for doubt or uncertainty. I gave myself a quick pep talk before I got out of my car to go inside the building. I reminded myself that there was something so much better waiting for me on the other side of this craziness. I was ready to start this journey for the last time.

I went in and signed my name on the sign-in sheet. The receptionist looked up from her paperwork and let out a loud scream of excitement, "Dana! Oh, my gosh! How are you, my dear?" I was totally embarrassed by this welcome, but then again, it put my mind at ease within minutes when the receptionist leaned in to tell me, "Don't you be ashamed about coming back. Unfortunately, we see this all the time. You are going to be fine. They're going to help to get you right back on track."

To my surprise, the receptionist buzzed me into the office area behind her. It turns out, I would need to go through another intake process in order to determine my needs and goals that I would start working on. My therapist, Petergay, was unavailable at that time, so my intake interview took place with a different therapist. I waited patiently as the intake therapist, Dave, ushered me into his office, told me to have a seat anywhere, and moved a comfy chair to sit across from me. Before Dave began asking questions, I was already crying. He gave me a few tissues from a Kleenex box located on a table to my right. The room was cozy with dim lighting. There was soft jazz music playing softly and there was the relaxing sound coming from this small rock-like waterfall that was sitting on his desk. I felt so at ease, but the tears were confusing. I had no idea at that moment why I couldn't stop crying. After a few short minutes, I took a few deep breaths, and I was ready to begin.

Dave introduced himself to me and let me know that his only goal was to get me set up on the right path. He shared with me that we would determine how much help I needed, and we would develop a plan that works specifically for me. I felt so much better hearing this and understanding that I was not alone. My intake interview lasted for 60 minutes, so after we were done, Dave walked me over to the group therapy room. There were still two hours left. Thankfully, the group was already taking their first 15-minute break, so I was able to enter the room while it was empty. I thanked Dave, and then I walked over to the coffee nook and fixed a cup of coffee. I knew I was beyond nervous because in addition to the coffee I had at the coffee shop, I also had two cups of coffee at home that morning while smoking a cigarette on my patio. My attempt at psyching myself up. I found a seat on the far wall of the room and picked up a copy of the Big Book that was on the chair. I sat down and tried to busy myself by rummaging through my purse. Before I could distract myself from looking around the room, Zola, one of the counselors came over to greet me. I stood up and Zola hugged me tightly. As soon as she embraced me, I burst into tears. I was, literally, shaking. One of the group members who I hadn't met yet, came over with a box of Kleenex. I thanked her and took several sheets from the box. I blew my nose and cleaned my face. Zola stood there rubbing my back. She asked me what happened, and I started to tell her about my relapse, suicide attempt, and hospitalization, but there was no time for that. Britt had walked in, and the group was ready to resume.

When Britt laid eyes on me, I could see the concern on his face. As if he were reading my mind, he settled the group down and directed his attention to me. Before I could protest, Britt was sharing with the group that I had been through the program before, and it was okay that I had been. Britt pointed out a few other people who had been back and forth. He included himself in that number, admitting that he, himself, had relapsed several times before sobriety stuck. That didn't make me feel better. He asked a couple of those individuals to share their story briefly. There were two women who spoke first and then a young man. I felt so much motivation flowing through the room as they shared how hard their individual struggles had been. Each story gave me hope. Their stories were full of ups and downs, but most of all, their presence in that room meant they were persevering and not giving up. To my surprise, Britt offered for me to share what brought me back to Breakthroughs and I did not hesitate to share the story of my relapse. It felt so good to speak freely and to unpack the feelings of guilt, shame, embarrassment, and regret. I shed a lot of tears as I spoke, but I managed to push through my voice trembling and snot pooling above my upper lip. A beautiful thing happened that day in group. I received so much feedback and encouragement from the people in that room (we were all broken souls helping one another mend, even if we weren't healed yet ourselves) and I also welcomed the constructive criticism. There were a lot of members who helped me to point out my mistakes and they were ready to hold me accountable for this next go-round. My biggest assignment at that time was to get to the root of what caused me to relapse. It didn't just happen, and I needed to do the work to avoid the pitfalls of an unstable sobriety journey. My individual therapy with Petergay was scheduled to start the next day and I was ready. I was committed to my journey.

I was immediately tested after group therapy ended that day. As soon as group was over, Britt pulled me aside and asked me if I had a game plan for the rest of my afternoon. The timing was perfect because I was highly distracted. There were thoughts of alcohol running through my mind and I was starting to freak out about how I was going to stay strong enough to pass by all those damn liquor stores on my way home. I was about to go into a panic right when Britt showed up and asked me that question. I shared with him that I was looking forward to picking my son up from school and taking him to Taekwondo practice. Britt was persistent and wanted to know my plans for the period I would be alone. I shared with him that my first in-person appointment with the psychiatrist would be that afternoon since I was an outpatient now. That would keep me busy until it was time to pick up my son. I was hopeful because I knew that I was positioning myself to get the most help that I could get. Affirmations are crucial in the beginning of any self-healing journey. Especially the sober journey.

My first psychiatrist's appointment was at this place called, The Center for Healthy Minds. I grabbed lunch before I made my way across town for my 2 p.m. appointment. I didn't wait long once I arrived, signed in, and took a seat in the cozy waiting room. A young man, named Brian, greeted me shortly after I had gotten comfortable in my seat. He asked me to follow him to his office. Brian was a Nurse Practitioner and he shared with me that I had the option to be seen by the head psychiatrist, however, he was booked out two whole months. I agreed to begin working with Brian because of my experience in the pharmaceutical industry, I knew that Nurse Practitioners and Physician's Assistants were just as qualified. Brian and I jumped right in!

The first part of my treatment with Brian involved walking through my history (medical, physical, emotional, mental, spiritual, etc.). We discussed how important it was for me to replace old coping skills with new ones. Brian committed to helping me to take my life back. First things, first: Diagnostic test to nail down my true diagnosis. That first appointment with Brian was pivotal in my treatment journey. Brian conducted a test where I had to answer several questions about my behavior and thought processes. I was floored when he handed me a check-off sheet where I had to put a check mark next to each statement that applied to me. If you've ever been given one of these questionnaires, you'll understand why I was in utter shock when I had checked off every single box on that list. I hadn't paid attention to the title or name of the test, so I looked up top to see if it was listed. There was no diagnosis listed, but I knew this couldn't be good. Once Brian reviewed the sheet carefully, he looked up at me and slowly stated these words, "It looks like you've been dealing with bipolar disorder."

I felt a wave of sadness, anger, relief, and then excitement! How is that possible? For me, it was confirmation and a complete explanation, as well as an understanding of my behavior over the past several years. For my entire life, I have always been hyper, and I've always been full of energy. There has always been a running joke about me with my family members and friends, they described me as a "spinning top" or the "Energizer Bunny". I've always assumed that I was blessed with an amazing amount of energy. But with that gift, comes the extreme opposite of that spectrum, which includes major depression. On top of this earth-shattering diagnosis, it explained why I had dealt with sleep challenges. I was able to look back over several years and see the cycles. The obvious loud difficulties that I was experiencing and ignoring to my detriment were evident looking in my rearview mirror. So was the impulsive behavior that I couldn't seem to control but made excuses for like promiscuity, dead-end relationships, and the inability to commit to anything long-term. There was so much more that came rushing at me in that moment. I let the tears fall from my eyes and I looked through the blur of this inexplicable waterfall as I cried out for Brian to, "HELP ME, PLEASE!"

Now that I had more answers, I was even more determined to fight back. Brian and I chiseled away at my treatment plan. We also discussed what medication treatment options were available to help me to manage the symptoms of bipolar disorder. I was open to this discussion because I was desperate to get my life back. So, over the course of the past several years, I maintained psychiatric appointments, I have had one-on-one therapy, I have taken my medication faithfully, I have gone to AA meetings, and I've implemented varying coping mechanisms to help deal with the stressors of life and manage my symptoms.

The unique thing about the symptoms of bipolar disorder is that you must work extremely hard to be in tune with your mood. I must constantly gauge whether my excitement is real, and I have had to learn how to channel my energy. When I restarted treatment, my body was slowly responding to the medication that I was being given. I was in group therapy one day (maybe by week 3); and suddenly, I was distracted by the idea of going to my favorite liquor store and getting my favorite vodka on the way home. It was so sunny and beautiful outside, and I wanted to be free! I wanted to say, "fuck it" and live my life. That day, I made it through group therapy and upon entering my car to leave, I called my tattoo artist. I asked if she had time to do two quick tattoos (one on each of my wrists). She told me to come through and as I drove to her shop, I decided on the two tattoos I wanted: Left inner wrist, "Live, Laugh, Love" inside of an infinity sign. My goal was to live my life to the fullest, to laugh at everything that came my way, and to love relentlessly. The right inner wrist: a Gemini symbol with the word "Gemini" written inside with flowers and a butterfly (my favorite). The symbol truly represented my personality at the time. Gemini is symbolized by twins representing the duality and neutrality that is inherent. I was fully accepting of who I was, yet I had no idea I was in one of my manic states. Need further proof? I left the tattoo shop and drove to a car dealership. Let's just say the day ended with me leaving that car dealership in my company car, followed by two dealership employees delivering my new Jeep Cherokee, purchased on a whim! They pulled into my driveway and handed me the keys. I thanked them and they went on their way.

With no rhyme or reason, I decided that I needed a personal vehicle and that's exactly what I got. There was no buyer's remorse or guilt later, and if it made sense to me in my bipolar brain, then that's all that mattered. I hadn't had a car payment or car insurance in years because my company provided those things. I DID NOT NEED another vehicle for any reason whatsoever. Here I was leaping into commitments and agreements that I had no business getting into, but I couldn't be stopped. I even sold the idea to my family members and friends once they found out I had purchased a vehicle. I ultimately started saying that it would be handed down to my son, who still had three more years before he would start driving. Having bipolar can be exhilarating when you're manic. My task was to find balance in my life, so once I shared with Brian what I had done, he helped me to regain my focus and develop ways to be aware of when I might be headed toward a manic episode.

Just like we can physically check our blood pressure, blood sugar, and cholesterol; we are responsible for checking our mental health, although it's not so easily measured. Typically, patients are given questionnaires that help determine a mental health diagnosis which are based on scales and point systems. I continued to go to group therapy and individual counseling at Breakthroughs over the next three months. I poured every ounce of my energy into working on solidifying and protecting my sobriety. I remember having to push through the anger I felt once I came to grips with the fact that I would NEVER be able to drink alcohol for the rest of my life. I felt angry because I couldn't understand how so many other people could control themselves and simply enjoy one glass of wine, or one beer, or one shot. I had to have it ALL and I had to learn to modify that way of thinking. Having bipolar truly makes you feel like everything is an "all or nothing" situation. Everything about what I learned that second time around in treatment centered around plugging into the right resources and not letting go. This battle is impossible to win alone so once I realized my mishaps, I was all in. There are some areas of my life that have been served well by having bipolar disorder. Unfortunately, the extreme depression that comes with it didn't serve me at all and almost caused my demise.

Please, believe me when I say those first three months were hell. I dealt with a mountain of emotional difficulties because fighting the urge to drink was extremely taxing. I had to find a way to keep myself busy. I was constantly trying to find things that gave me motivation. I started a page on Facebook that was specifically designed to put a positive spin on addressing issues related to mental health. I knew from my years of working as a therapist, that there was this negative stigma around mental illness. I formed a community of people who were on the same mission – to stay positive and motivated enough to face our challenges. The page has grown over the years. I call it "Promoting Positive Mental Health".

I also created a hash tag, #choosehappiness, to encourage others to choose their mood each day. Although I was battling bipolar/depression, I forced myself to choose my mood each morning. This was crucial for me. I always started my day with a prayer and believe me it took prayer to continue to take all the different medications I was given. I felt so embarrassed by this, yet, each day, I chose to comply and be an active participant in my healing and sober journey. I never quite found the right AA group, so my therapist and I discussed ways to strengthen my sobriety. I did a ton of workbook activities that she assigned to me, and I continued to attend the AA group on Wednesdays that met at Breakthroughs, right after group therapy. I felt more comfortable in this group, so I decided to at least give myself a fighting chance, not to mention, attending AA meetings was a required part of my treatment plan so I needed to get this done.

My individual therapy appointments were brutal at times. My therapist was amazing at pulling out the gunk and the dirt buried so deep within me. I cried so much in those sessions. I hate crying, so that was a big deal. I was able to pinpoint the various times in my life where I didn't even try to fight. I worked through the thoughts that had caused me to be a perfectionist all my life. I also took a deep dive into my impulsivity when it came to men. I had gotten so far from the idea of having a meaningful, healthy relationship that I had to start from ground zero in terms of learning to love myself, first. No more giving myself to anyone who does not have my best interest at heart. In the beginning of my treatment, I decided to stay single for a while, which is also something most treatment programs recommend, as well, if you're not married.

I think that's when I was able to truly have a breakthrough. I learned to love myself and accept myself, flaws, and all. I learned to do the daily affirmations and I mastered the art of looking in the mirror and speaking my truth. Over time, I developed the best and most effective coping skills for me, as well as positive habits. It is, literally, my lifestyle to stay positive, active, and motivated. I now live in my truth.

One thing that really helped me in the beginning was when I picked up the manuscript of the book that I had been writing three years prior to my meltdown. I love writing and it only took one session to get back at it. I look back in amazement and I'm beyond proud of myself for cranking out my first book within three months of being released from the hospital. I was admitted on May 31st and my book was officially published on August 12th that same year. I planned and coordinated the biggest book signing party for November 12th (the birthday of my baby brother who had passed away in 2010 at the age of 25). My first book was a novella based on the lives of the women in my life, as well as my own life. I poured into this story and created a complicated character who triumphed in the end. The moral of the story was that we all wear a mask and when we are brave enough to remove it, we're able to live in the truth of we really are. (That also became a hash tag on my social media platforms: #LiveinTruth.)

Life in recent years has been rewarding in so many ways, however, I still have my share of trials. I'm in a place now where

I know exactly what to do to protect my peace and my sobriety. I must make a conscious choice each day to be optimistic and shift my thoughts throughout the day, as needed. I also must recommit to myself daily. I owe that to myself, and I can finally say that I love who I am, and I love my story. I love the journey that I have been on, which has led me right here.

Chapter 11

New Life

So, where am I today? What does my life look like now? What are the major changes that I've had to adjust to? As of 2024, the completion of this book, I am eight years into my sobriety, and I must admit, I still must choose this lifestyle each morning that I open my eyes. I choose to stay present. My son is an amazing adult and has a bachelor's degree in film production. I would have never been able to see this beautiful blessing if I had thrown in the towel and succeeded at death in 2016. I'm thankful that my relationship with my son is more solid than ever. He has always been my biggest fan. We talk daily and I constantly monitor his mood, even if he doesn't. We've had tough conversations about my mental health and addiction over the years, and he has witnessed me make tremendous strides. He has grown to trust me again. I have tried to instill so many values in my son and I'm starting to see the fruits of my labor.

My son's father and I are cordial today. There is no hate and no blaming going on. We successfully co-parented our son into his adult life, and I think we both did a great job with making things work, no matter how painful it was. We check in with each other from time to time and we make sure we're always on the same page with our adult son. Some might find that strange, but this type of parenting has worked for us and our son and as long as we stay connected, we know that our son will benefit the most. To get where we are as his parents took sacrifice and a whole lot of "come to Jesus" meetings, but we continue to survive.

I have kept my focus on my healing, and I have accepted the truth of who I am. Part of that meant learning how to cope with the major stressors in my life. A lot of my stress came from my job, so I started to work on my exit strategy from the pharmaceutical sales industry. Although my sights were set on escaping Corporate America, I still put forth my best effort and ended up becoming a top performing sales representative. I won several awards, including a seven-day, all-expense paid trip to Hawaii (two years in a row)! I have beautiful plaques and trophies. I proved to myself that I had it in me to be an amazing sales rep, but over time I realized that was not my place. It simply was not my passion. Many of my concerns were centered around finding what makes me happy. Once I was sober and could see clearly, I had to come to grips with the fact that I was not living out my passion. I was selling my soul for a pair of diamond handcuffs. The lifestyle that this profession provided stared me straight in the eyes and I was up against the wall. Would I practice what I was preaching? The whole idea of "living in truth"? Could I practice the whole idea of a healthy work/life balance? I played the game for years because I was afraid of what was out there. Where would I get this type of money, this much flexibility, all the perks? Not in the field of psychology and social work, that's for sure! So, I continued to do the work and I continued to dream. I continued to set my sight high, and I found myself doing what comes so natural for me. I was coaching people, helping others break into the industry, and promoting positive mental health on my social media sites. That was (and is) my passion. God was up to something. I eagerly started to share my story on my social media platforms, pouring every ounce of myself into shattering the negative ideas around mental health issues/illnesses, and addictions. I was so loud with my message, and I had no shame: "Hi, my name is Dana, and I'm an alcoholic."

C H A P T E R   1 2

New Beginnings

I was forced to adjust and adapt to a new normal while writing this book. I have been writing it for a long time, while still in treatment (up until 2022), and still seeing my mental health professionals. I am proud to say that I no longer have a need for medication to treat bipolar or depression at the time of completing this book. I worked closely with my treatment team to get to where I am mentally. I also keep a strict regimen when it comes to my physical activity and my food intake. I stay away from the things that agitate me or annoy me and I work extra hard to keep my stress levels down. I walk every morning with my dog, Pinot Grigio (are you even surprised at his name)? He joined our family in 2018. I also dance every day for at least 30 minutes to some of my favorite music, which is extremely therapeutic for me.

With all of those pluses happening, I would have never guessed in a million years I'd face the biggest test of my sobriety ever! I was laid off on May 5, 2022, after 15 years with the pharmaceutical company I was with. I took the summer of 2022 off and was then hired by another company in September 2022. Would you believe I was laid off again, April 11, 2023, after only eight months! My world felt like it was shaken upside down again. My son wisely pointed out something I didn't initially consider. He said, "Mom, you've been laid off two times within a one-year period. Don't you think God might be trying to tell you something?" I love my son for his intuitiveness and his bluntness.

I had been dreaming of my life coaching and consulting business for years. I was also ready to start my motivational speaking engagements. It's as if God spoke directly to me because shortly after my transition out of the pharmaceutical world, I received a phone call from a friend inviting me to be the keynote speaker at a Mother's Day banquet in a city near my hometown. I was planning to visit my mother that weekend anyway, so that was perfect. I remember my sister, Latricia, who is also my best friend, making sure I was mentally prepared to speak, since I was recently unemployed. Something in my gut told me to accept the invitation. Preparing that speech really helped me to get through an initial rough patch. I am so glad I committed myself to the assignment because that was the day, Saturday, May 13, 2023, when I came alive. I felt the blood pulsating throughout my body as I shared my story with young mothers. I talked about the depths of healing that needs to take place in each of us. I talked about what I've learned, and I poured into those women from a cup that was finally running over. I had finally positioned myself exactly where I needed to be. There were many tears shed that day. There were hugs exchanged, and private stories whispered in my ear. So many people said, "thank you." One mother pulled me aside and shared with me that as a result of sharing my story, her young adult daughter leaned over to her during my talk and whispered that she had those same thoughts a couple of weeks ago. I was able to point them in the right direction. These women reminded me of my calling. It is spiritual and it is healing. My cup continued to overflow, and I walked away still full. It was confirmation that I had something of impact to bring to the table.

That next day was Mothers' Day and my brother, JoJo, was visiting from California, my other brother, Eric, came up from Ft. Lauderdale, and my sister, Latricia, who lives locally was there, as well. My mom had all her living kids with her on Mother's Day weekend, 2023. Little did we know so much change was on the horizon and that last get-together would come to mean so much.

A few short weeks after Mother's Day, I was in Jamaica with plans to finish this book. I had the most amazing time from the moment I landed in Montego Bay that Sunday, May 28th. I woke up bright and early each morning, fixed my coffee and sat on my patio to write. It was an amazing feeling to be in my favorite place with no interruptions. It was me and my thoughts. I reminded myself to have fun, of course, so trust me when I say you'll want to check out my next book where the topic will be all things being single, dating, and relationships. So, we'll stick a pin in the shenanigans I got into while celebrating the week of my 45th birthday (which was primarily my reason for this solo trip in the first place). At any rate, by that Thursday morning, I was on the phone with my mom and dad, individually. They both sang horrible renditions of happy birthday songs and we laughed until we were sore. That was the last time I would hear my mother's voice because the next morning, she posted her final post on Facebook: "God is a good God; Come by here, Lord." That was it. I saw it from my room in Jamaica where I had been up writing and enjoying room service. I hit the "love" button as I did every morning after my mom's sentimental shout out to God. I came to a nice stopping point with my writing and decided to share the title of this book on my social media platforms. I posted the rough draft's title and sat back with a smile on my face (almost done). Not even an hour later, I got the call that flipped my world upside down.

My thoughts seemed jumbled because I could have sworn, I heard my sister, Latricia, say, "Mommy had a heart attack, Dana. She didn't make it." I couldn't comprehend what my sister was saying so I kept trying to catch my breath so I could hear her more clearly. I kept saying, "no, this is a joke, right?" I wanted to know why she was saying those words. I fell to my knees and screamed the most gripping and agonizing cry. I didn't recognize my own voice. I never wanted to hear or feel that type of scream coming from my own body. How could this be happening? And today? The day AFTER my birthday? I asked my sister what kind of sick joke this was, and she helped me to calm down. I immediately asked about my dad and my other siblings. I knew that my sister had to make more painful phone calls to Eric, in Ft. Lauderdale, and JoJo, out in California. We hurried off the phone so she could muster up the strength to make those calls while I immediately started working on getting the first flight out of Jamaica. My mom was dead, and I was on an island by my damn self, surrounded by alcohol. I can't lie, it took every ounce of strength for me to allow myself to feel this impossible pain. The first several hours were the worst because I couldn't get a flight out until the next afternoon. I had to pull out all the stops. I was on the phone with my siblings and my dad more than ever. That was the last time I slept over the next month. My life was in a tailspin, and I couldn't make it stop.

The remainder of that Friday, June 2nd, I kept myself busy by walking the resort property and along the beach. I took occasional breaks and found myself zoned out staring off at the beautiful ocean. I remember thinking about how precious and sweet my mother was. I felt her gentle spirit all around me that day and I welcomed that feeling. It was comforting to imagine her smile. I can't tell you how I got from Friday to finally landing in Florida that Saturday evening. All I remember is that when the plane landed, I started to hyperventilate and could not seem to catch my breath. I was in the last row at the back of the plane. As I took deep breaths, I would breathe out and the sound leaving my body was heartbreaking. It was a cry of deep hurt and pain. I was trying so hard to control my emotions, but that was making it worse. One of the flight attendants knew about my mom since I had asked for permission to sit in the back row because I needed as much space as I could get. Thankfully, there were two empty rows, and I was able to get comfortable with my feet on the seats and my head leaned back. I hadn't cried at all that day, but for some reason, once the flight touched down, I lost it. The flight attendant came to me and rubbed my back. Her calm voice softly repeated, "it's going to be okay."

As if all this drama wasn't already enough, once I got home, I took a Covid-19 test. My throat felt funny, and I felt as if I was coming down with something. My test came back positive, and

I almost passed out. I yelled up to God, "You have GOT to be kidding me!!! This can't happen right now!" Earlier in the week, while still in Jamaica, I had a hard time getting comfortable in my room because of the extreme heat outside and the constant blowing of the air conditioner on the inside. It was either too hot or too cold in my room. A recipe for disaster but I wasn't about to ruin my trip. I had gone to the gift shop by that Tuesday to load up on some cold medications just in case. Now, here I was standing in my bathroom with tears streaming down my face. If I couldn't make it to my mother's funeral, I knew I would die. I got online to see the protocol and was relieved to see that it looked as if I'd only need five days of isolation; and I would need to wear a KN95 mask if I had to be around people. I called my dad and siblings and let them know about my test results. I took the next few days to nurse myself back to health. Thankfully, I was still able to help with the funeral arrangements to a certain extent. I was on a conference call with my family and the funeral director that Monday morning, but I must admit, I can't tell you the first thing that was said. I was so woozy and lightheaded from the medications. I wasn't sleeping or eating at all, so I felt discombobulated. At some point, I just pressed end and got off the call. I couldn't take it. I think the most painful responsibility I had was to select the photos for my mom's obituary. That's what I get for always being the one to capture photos and videos when our family is together. Thankfully, I have a million pictures of my beautiful mom, so the only problem I faced was narrowing it down to the best ones. I was able to get home that Thursday. The wake was on that Friday evening. The funeral was on that Saturday. At some point after both memorial events, I woke up in my own bed facing my new normal. This was truly a new beginning whether I wanted it or not.

Grieving the loss of my job and the loss of my mom also meant deciding what was next for me. I had interviewed with a great pharmaceutical company prior to my trip to Jamaica, I received a denial letter from them the week I returned from vacation. Everything was crashing down around me, and the losses were continuing. The irony. I was quickly starting to build up enough confidence to make the leap I had been praying about for years. Less than one month after laying my mom to rest, I decided to finally dive into the entrepreneur pool, and I got my Limited Liability Company approved and launched my life coaching and consulting business: ***Live in Truth Life Coaching & Consulting.*** My dream came true!

My dating life has remained unremarkable. I've continued a healing journey that is doing my heart well! I'm more than convinced that a healthy, strong, fabulous relationship awaits me in my future. I am learning so much about myself and I am eager to share the beautiful person that has always lived inside of me. I have a strong relationship with God, and I trust Him wholeheartedly for whatever is next for me. This story is getting easier and easier to share and I know that this message is for AT LEAST ONE PERSON! That's my prayer.

I am currently working on my third book and growing my business. My mom's abrupt passing catapulted me to commit to living out the latter years of my life exactly the way I've always dreamed and imagined. I am a full-time author, a life coach, sober (from alcohol) and I'm free. I allow myself to feel the waves of pain and sorrow that come crashing occasionally. But for the most part, my heart is happy. I feel joy. I have learned to take one step at a time and that's exactly how I plan to move forward. No rush. There is no better place to be than to live in the truth of who I am based on how God sees me. I am fearless and bold. Whether I feel happiness or not is not up to others and I have accepted that. That's why each day, I get moving, no matter how I feel. Every day I decide to #choosehappiness and to #liveintruth on this #soberjourney. I can honestly say that I love my crazy, beautiful life, with all its perfect imperfections!